HOW TO START A PROPERTY MANAGEMENT BUSINESS

Attract Top Tenants, Maximize Profits, and Achieve Peace of Mind

Jeanelle K. Douglas

Copyright © 2024 by Jeanelle K. Douglas.

All rights reserved. No part of this book, How To Start a Property Management Business, *may be reproduced, stored in a retrieval system, or transmitted in any form or by any means, electronic, mechanical, photocopying, recording, or otherwise, without the prior written permission of the author, Jeanelle K. Douglas.*

Contents

Introduction 7
    Definition of Property Management. 9
    The importance of property management businesses ... 13
    Property Management Industry Overview 16
    Scope and Opportunities 19
Understanding the Property Management Industry 23
    Market Analysis 26
    Current Trends 29
    Market Size and Growth 32
    Competitive Analysis 41
    Legal and Regulatory Landscape 44
    Legal Frameworks for Maintaining Compliance 48
Conducting a Feasibility Study 53
    Assessing Personal and Financial Readiness 57
    Identifying Potential Risks and Challenges 60
    Financial Projections and Budgeting 63
    Creating a Business Plan 67

    Legal considerations 70

        Business Structure 75

        Sole proprietorship. 79

        Limited Liability Companies (LLC) 83

        Corporation 87

        Licenses and Permits 90

        Insurance Requirements 93

        Contracts and Agreements 97

Setting Up Your Property Management Business 101

        Location and Office Setup 106

        Equipment and Technology 110

        Staff Requirements 114

        Establishing professional networks 118

        Developing Services and Pricing 121

        Property Maintenance 124

        Tenant Screening and Placement 127

        Rent Collection. 130

        Eviction Service 134

Other Value-Added Services 138

Pricing Strategy 141

Marketing and branding 145

Establishing a brand identity 149

Online Presence 153

Traditional Marketing Strategies 157

Networking and partnerships 161

Client Testimonials and Reviews 164

Traditional marketing strategies 168

Networking and Partnerships 172

Client Testimonials and Reviews 176

Compliance and Risk Management 180

Fair Housing Laws 184

Environmental Regulations 187

Data Security and Privacy 191

Strategies for Risk Mitigation 195

Chapter 10 200

Building Client Relationships 200

Managing Complaints and Issues 209

Chapter 11 212

Scaling Your Property Management Business 212

Expansion Strategies 215

Chapter 12 226

Staying informed and adapting to changes 226

Industry Updates and Trends 229

Adapting to Market Changes 234

Introduction

This book titled How to Start a Property Management Business is your full guide to going on a profitable path in the dynamic world of property management. Whether you're an experienced real estate professional wishing to extend your services or a fledgling entrepreneur with a love for property, this book will provide you with the information, tools, and tactics you need to start and build a successful property management business.

Property management is a diverse sector with a critical function in the real estate ecosystem. Landlords and property owners rely on trained management specialists to handle day-to-day operations, optimize investment returns, and assure tenant happiness, whether in residential complexes or commercial buildings. With the growing demand for rental properties and the changing landscape of property ownership, the prospects for property management companies are numerous and diversified.

In this book, we will go over every step of beginning and running a property management business, from performing a feasibility study and overcoming legal issues to designing services, promoting your firm, and scaling for growth. Whether you're starting out as a single operator or want to establish a profitable business, our step-by-step approach will offer you concrete insights and practical assistance for navigating the hurdles and capitalizing on the possibilities in the property management sector.

This book contains real-world examples, case studies, and expert recommendations from seasoned experts to inspire and guide you on your entrepreneurial path. Whether you want to build a portfolio of properties under management, establish yourself as a trusted advisor in your community, or use technology to streamline operations, "How to Start a Property Management Business" will be your trusted guide, providing valuable insights and strategies to help you succeed in this dynamic and rewarding industry.

So, whether you're ready to dive into property management or want to improve your current business processes, let's go on this exciting adventure together to maximize the potential of your property management firm.

Definition of Property Management.

Starting a property management company involves entering a complex sector focused on efficiently and successfully administering various types of real estate assets. Property management is about developing vibrant communities, boosting asset value, and ensuring the pleasure of both property owners and tenants.

Property management includes a variety of responsibilities and actions aimed at preserving, running, and increasing the value of real estate assets. It entails the strategic management of residential, commercial, and industrial assets, such as apartment buildings, office complexes, retail spaces, and others.

At the core of it all property managers are dedicated in bridging the gap between property owners and renters, allowing for seamless and pleasant interactions while protecting both sides' interests. Property managers serve as middlemen, acting as renters' principal point of contact while also representing property owners' interests.

Keeping properties in good condition is one of the most important components of property management. This involves regular maintenance, repairs, and renovations to keep buildings safe, functional, and visually appealing. Managers may save on costly repairs and protect asset value in the long run by being proactive with property upkeep.

In addition to physical upkeep, property management includes financial management chores. This includes rent collection, budgeting, accounting, and financial reporting. Property managers are in charge of determining suitable rental rates, collecting payments, and handling all financial activities relating to the property.

Tenant management is another important aspect of property management. This includes screening potential renters, leasing unoccupied apartments, resolving tenant complaints, and enforcing leases.

Effective tenant management is critical for building positive connections and guaranteeing tenant satisfaction, which leads to tenant retention and a consistent income stream for property owners.

Property management goes beyond day-to-day operations and includes strategic planning and decision-making. Property managers must tailor detailed management plans to meet the specific needs and goals of each property. This may entail establishing investment goals, formulating a marketing strategy, and implementing measures to increase property value and recruit excellent renters.

It also, necessitates staying up-to-date on legal and regulatory regulations governing real estate properties. This involves knowledge of landlord-tenant laws, building rules, zoning regulations, and other applicable legislation. Compliance with these rules is critical for reducing risks and avoiding legal obligations.

Property managers must be excellent communicators in order to deal effectively with property owners, renters, vendors, and other stakeholders.

Building good connections based on trust and professionalism is critical for maintaining a favorable reputation and obtaining repeat business in the competitive property management market.

Additionally, technology is becoming increasingly vital in modern property management organizations. Property management software, internet platforms, and digital technologies help to streamline procedures, increase efficiency, and improve communication with customers and renters. Embracing technology allows property managers to stay organized, streamline productivity, and deliver a consistent experience for all parties.

Beginning a property management company entails negotiating a complicated terrain of duties that includes physical maintenance, financial administration, tenant relations, strategic planning, legal compliance, communication, and technological integration. By understanding the multidimensional nature of property management and taking a complete approach to business operations, prospective property managers can develop a profitable and long-term business that benefits both property owners and renters.

The importance of property management businesses

Property management companies play an important role in the real estate industry, offering essential services that contribute to the functioning, sustainability, and profitability of buildings. These enterprises perform a complicated role that goes well beyond simple administrative activities, comprising a wide range of obligations critical to the proper operation and upkeep of real estate assets.

These companies are primarily responsible for maintaining and increasing the value of properties. Property managers keep buildings and rental units beautiful, functional, and in good shape by performing regular maintenance, planned renovations, and responsive upkeep. This not only protects property owners' long-term investment worth but also improves renters' quality of life and adds to the community's general appeal.

They play an important role in developing beneficial connections between landlords and tenants. Property managers serve as the primary point of contact, allowing for clear communication, rapid resolution of complaints, and fair enforcement of lease terms. This develops trust and mutual respect among parties, resulting in improved tenant satisfaction, increased tenant retention rates, and, ultimately, a more stable and profitable investment for property owners.

Property management companies take the lead role in ensuring legal compliance and regulatory requirements in the real estate market. Property managers remain up-to-date on the latest laws, rules, and ordinances affecting landlord-tenant interactions, building requirements, safety standards, and other issues. By adhering to these regulatory standards, property managers reduce risks and liabilities and protect the interests of both property owners and renters.

Property management firms play a crucial role in the real estate industry. These businesses serve a comprehensive function that goes far beyond administrative activities, comprising obligations critical to protecting property value, developing healthy relationships, ensuring legal compliance, and contributing to community life. Aspiring entrepreneurs in the property management industry must appreciate the importance of their enterprises and aim to provide great service that benefits property owners, renters, and communities.

Property Management Industry Overview

The property management business is a dynamic and varied real estate sector that provides a wide variety of services and activities aimed at properly managing and enhancing the value of real estate assets. The property management sector includes a wide range of property types, from residential apartment complexes to commercial office spaces and industrial buildings, and it serves a variety of stakeholders, including property owners, renters, investors, and communities.

At its foundation, the property management sector is motivated by the desire to bridge the gap between property owners and renters, promote smooth interactions, and ensure property operations run seamlessly. Property management businesses act as intermediaries, covering a wide range of chores and responsibilities such as property maintenance, tenant interactions, financial administration, and regulatory compliance.

One of the property management sector's distinguishing characteristics is its ability to adapt and respond to market trends and changes in the real estate environment. To effectively negotiate the industry's intricacies and fulfill the changing demands of property owners and renters, property managers must remain up-to-date on developing market circumstances, demographic shifts, and regulatory developments.

Property management businesses not only serve as operational custodians of real estate assets, but they also play an important role in boosting investment returns and increasing profitability for property owners. Property managers may assist property owners in accomplishing their financial goals and maximizing the value of their real estate assets by applying strategic management techniques, using technology, and staying current on market trends. Property managers in the property management sector frequently possess specific knowledge in real estate law, finance, marketing, and customer service, showcasing a high level of professionalism and skill.

As a result, beginning a property management company necessitates a thorough awareness of the market environment, a commitment to continuous learning and professional growth, and a commitment to providing great service to customers.

Property management market provides several prospects for budding entrepreneurs seeking to launch their own businesses. With the right combination of industry knowledge, business acumen, and a customer-centric approach, entrepreneurs can build successful property management businesses that not only meet the needs of property owners and tenants but also contribute to the overall growth and vibrancy of the real estate industry.

Scope and Opportunities

The breadth and potential of the property management market are enormous and diverse, providing ambitious entrepreneurs with a plethora of options to pursue and profit from. As the real estate industry evolves and expands, the need for expert property management services has never been higher, offering an ideal environment for new enterprises to develop and prosper.

The most significant opportunities in the property management sector is the sheer number of properties that require management services. The diversity of property types, which range from residential apartment buildings and single-family houses to commercial office spaces, retail centers, and industrial complexes, allows for plenty of specialization and specialty targeting. Entrepreneurs might target certain property types or market niches depending on their interests, experience, and local market dynamics.

The growing trend towards property investment and rental property ownership has increased the need for expert property management services. Many property owners, especially those who own many properties or live far away from their rental homes, understand the need to delegate property management chores to competent specialists. This creates a tremendous potential for property management companies to provide bespoke solutions that address the specific requirements and preferences of property owners, resulting in long-term relationships and recurring income streams.

To add to the growing trend, the growth of technology and digital tools has transformed the property management industry, creating new potential for innovation and efficiency. Property management software, internet platforms, and mobile applications have made administrative processes easier, improved communication with customers and renters, and increased overall operating efficiencies.

Entrepreneurs joining the property management sector may use these technology improvements to distinguish their services, optimize productivity, and provide more value to clients.

Also, the increased emphasis on sustainability and eco-friendly practices in the real estate industry has generated possibilities for property management firms to provide value-added services that prioritize energy efficiency, waste reduction, and environmental stewardship.

Businesses that incorporate sustainable methods into their property management operations can not only save operating costs but also attract environmentally aware customers and renters that value sustainability in their real estate decisions. And the changing regulatory landscape in the real estate market creates both obstacles and possibilities for property management companies.

Property managers may position themselves as trustworthy consultants to property owners by remaining up-to-date on changes in landlord-tenant legislation, building codes, and other pertinent regulations. This knowledge of regulatory compliance may be a useful selling point for property management companies looking to differentiate themselves in a competitive market.

Understanding the Property Management Industry

The property management business is a vibrant and varied segment of the real estate market. Understanding the complexities of this market is critical for entrepreneurs trying to launch a property management company. It entails understanding market trends, selecting target markets, assessing rivals, and navigating the legal and regulatory framework. Having a thorough grasp of the property management sector necessitates an extensive examination of market trends and dynamics.

This includes looking into crucial factors, including vacancy rates, rental costs, demographic trends, and economic circumstances. Understanding market trends enables entrepreneurs to discover development possibilities and modify their company strategies to meet rising market demands.

Understanding the property management market helps in defining target audiences as well as their individual requirements and preferences. Individual property owners, real estate investors, homeowners' organizations, and commercial property developers all benefit from property management services. Understanding each target audience's distinct demands and pain points allows entrepreneurs to adjust their service offerings and marketing tactics to effectively meet their clients' needs and differentiate themselves in the market.

Additionally, studying rivals is an important part of understanding the property management sector. By doing a thorough competition study, entrepreneurs may learn about the strengths and shortcomings of current property management firms in their target industry. This includes analyzing rivals' service offerings, pricing methods, consumer feedback, and market positioning. Entrepreneurs can differentiate their firm and carve out a position in the competitive landscape by identifying market gaps and areas where rivals may fall short.

This profession necessitates in navigating the legal and regulatory structures that govern real estate and property management activities. This includes being acquainted with landlord-tenant laws, fair housing rules, building codes, zoning ordinances, and other applicable legislation. Compliance with these rules is critical for preserving the interests of property owners and renters while avoiding potential legal penalties. Entrepreneurs beginning a property management firm must ensure that their operations follow all applicable rules and regulations in order to maintain ethical business practices and earn customer confidence.

Market Analysis

To begin the road to starting a property management firm, entrepreneurs must undertake a thorough market study to understand the present environment and find areas for development and difference. Market analysis is the process of acquiring and evaluating data on the real estate market, demographic trends, competition, and client preferences in order to guide strategic decision-making and corporate planning.

First and foremost, conducting a market study requires a thorough understanding of the local housing market. This includes looking at important factors, including average rental prices, vacancy rates, sales trends, and property appreciation rates. Examining these indicators, businesses may gain insight into the overall health and dynamics of their target area's real estate market, which is critical for predicting demand for property management services. Market analysis entails identifying and understanding the target audience for property management services.

This group comprises property owners, real estate investors, homeowners' organizations, and commercial property developers. Understanding the specific wants, interests, and pain points of each target audience group allows entrepreneurs to adjust their service offerings and marketing tactics to effectively answer their clients' demands and differentiate themselves in the market.

However, completing a competitive analysis is critical for understanding the competitive environment and identifying areas for differentiation. This entails researching current property management firms in the target market and examining their service offerings, pricing tactics, client feedback, and market positioning. Entrepreneurs can differentiate their businesses and attract customers by identifying market gaps and areas where rivals may be falling short.

Market study requires, looking at demographic changes and customer preferences that may influence demand for property management services.

This covers population growth, household demographics, lifestyle preferences, and employment trends.

Understanding these demographic trends enables entrepreneurs to identify target demographics with a high demand for property management services and tailor their marketing efforts to reach these audiences more effectively.

A well-executed market study lays the groundwork for a thriving property management company by finding chances for development and distinction in the competitive real estate industry.

Current Trends

In the ever-changing property management environment, staying current on trends is critical for entrepreneurs intending to launch a property management firm. These trends shape the sector while also providing significant insights into forthcoming possibilities and problems. Understanding and exploiting current trends allows entrepreneurs to position their firms for success and stay ahead of the curve in the competitive property management sector.

One noticeable development in the property management sector is the growing use of technology and digital tools to streamline operations and improve the client experience. Property management software, internet platforms, and mobile apps have transformed the way property managers interact with customers and renters, manage rental properties, and handle administrative work. These technological innovations not only increase productivity and accuracy but also provide more convenience and accessibility to customers and renters, resulting in improved satisfaction and retention rates.

Another prominent development in property management is an increased emphasis on sustainability and environmentally friendly techniques. With growing concern about environmental concerns and climate change, property managers are implementing green initiatives into their operations to decrease energy usage and waste and promote sustainability. This involves installing energy-efficient appliances, using environmentally friendly materials in home improvements, and applying sustainable landscaping methods. Property management companies that prioritize sustainability not only contribute to environmental protection but also attract environmentally aware customers and renters that respect sustainability in their real estate decisions.

The sharing economy's growth has had a significant impact on the property management sector. The growth of short-term rental platforms such as Air bnb and VRBO has offered new options for property owners to earn money from their properties through short-term rentals. As a result, property management companies are tailoring their services to this growing market sector, offering specialized services such as vacation rental management, guest screening, and short-term rental property upkeep. Property management companies may diversify their revenue sources by entering the sharing economy and capitalizing on the lucrative short-term rental market.

Also, the COVID-19 pandemic has accelerated several developments in the property management industry, particularly in the areas of remote employment and virtual property management. With the rise of remote work and digital communication, property managers are increasingly using virtual tools and platforms to conduct property tours, perform lease signings, and communicate with customers and renters remotely. This shift toward virtual property management not only increases flexibility and convenience, but it also improves safety and health measures in the aftermath of the epidemic. As remote work gains popularity, property management companies are poised to embrace virtual property management as a permanent fixture in the sector, providing new opportunities to adapt and thrive in the digital era.

Finally, entrepreneurs intending to launch a property management firm must remain up-to-date on current trends. Understanding and utilizing trends like technology improvements, environmental efforts, the sharing economy, and virtual property management may help entrepreneurs position their firms for success and capitalize on new possibilities in the dynamic property management market.

Market Size and Growth

Understanding the market size and development potential is critical for entrepreneurs entering the property management industry. The property management business is a substantial and quickly developing industry, fueled by factors such as urbanization, population expansion, and rising demand for rental homes.

First, consider the market size of the property management sector. Property management covers a wide range of properties, including residential, commercial, and industrial real estate. According to market research estimates, the worldwide property management industry is valued at billions of dollars every year and is expected to continue increasing gradually in the next few years. Factors contributing to this expansion include an increase in the number of rental properties, rising urbanization rates, and an increased need for professional property management services.

The property management business is experiencing strong growth, fueled by rising demand for rental units. With shifting demographic trends and lifestyle preferences, more people and families are choosing to rent rather than buy property. This trend is especially pronounced among younger generations, such as millennials and Generation Z, who value freedom and mobility. As a result, demand for rental properties is likely to rise further, necessitating the use of professional property management services to effectively manage these rental properties.

Therefore, the surge in real estate investment is creating growth opportunities for the property management business. The increasing popularity of real estate investing among individual investors, institutional investors, and real estate investment trusts (REITs) is driving the growing demand for property management services. Property management companies play an important role in increasing returns on investment for property owners by successfully managing and optimizing the performance of their real estate assets.

Technological advancements are transforming and driving the property management business forward. Property management software, internet platforms, and digital technologies have simplified administrative processes, improved communication, and increased operational efficiency in property management firms.

This technological breakthrough not only boosts productivity and cost-effectiveness, but it also provides new potential for property management companies to expand their operations and reach a larger customer base.

As customer tastes shift and market dynamics change, the property management sector is expected to expand further. As demographic shifts and lifestyle trends transform the real estate sector, property management companies may tailor their services to match the changing demands of customers and renters.

The growing emphasis on convenience and efficiency among property owners and renters is a major driver of the property management industry's growth. With hectic schedules and demanding lives becoming the norm, property owners are increasingly relying on professional property management services to handle their day-to-day ownership obligations. Similarly, tenants want hassle-free renting experiences and appreciate the ease of having a proactive property management company that can handle their problems quickly.

The emergence of specialty markets and specialized services is propelling the property management industry forward. As the real estate market grows increasingly divided and diverse, property management companies will be able to cater to certain market niches and provide specialized services customized to the unique demands of their clients.

The growing emphasis on client experience and satisfaction is propelling growth in the property management business. As renters become more discriminating and demanding, property management companies must prioritize customer service and satisfaction in order to retain tenants and attract new clients.

This includes responding to inquiries and maintenance requests in a timely manner, establishing clear communication channels, and delivering value-added services that improve renters' overall renting experience.

Property management business benefits from legislative reforms and policy measures aimed at raising housing standards and encouraging sustainable development. As governments and regulatory agencies tighten requirements and incentives for housing quality, energy efficiency, and environmental sustainability, property management companies may position themselves as leaders in compliance and sustainability. By implementing best practices and supporting sustainability initiatives, property management companies can differentiate themselves in the market and attract clients who value ethical and environmentally sensitive property management operations.

Targeted Audience

The target audience is an important component of starting a property management firm since it allows entrepreneurs to personalize their services to their clients' individual requirements and preferences. The target audience for property management services includes a wide range of people and organizations involved in real estate ownership, leasing, or management.

Individual property owners make up an important component of the target audience for property management companies. These may include homeowners who hold rental homes as investments, landlords with many rental units, or those who have inherited properties and need professional management assistance.

Individual property owners frequently lack the time, skill, or willingness to undertake the day-to-day obligations of property management, making them prime clients for property management firms.

In addition to individual property owners, property management companies cater to real estate investors and investment groups. These might include institutional investors, private equity firms, real estate investment trusts (REITs), and other companies that hold or manage real estate assets. Real estate investors often seek expert property management services to enhance investment returns, reduce risks, and assure their portfolios' long-term profitability.

Property management companies cater to commercial property owners and developers that own or manage commercial real estate assets such as office buildings, retail complexes, and industrial sites. Commercial property owners frequently require specialist property management services designed to meet the specific demands of commercial tenants, such as lease negotiations, tenant upgrades, and property upkeep.

They target homeowners' organizations (HOAs) and condominium associations, which manage and maintain common spaces and facilities in residential communities. HOAs and condominium organizations rely on property management services to conduct administrative work, enforce community rules and regulations, and maintain the overall community.

These companies may target certain segments of the real estate sector, such as vacation rental owners, student housing operators, or affordable housing providers. Specialist property management services must customize their offerings to meet the particular demands and preferences of these niche markets.

Additionally, property management companies may target homeowners who own holiday rentals or second homes. These owners frequently use professional management companies to handle reservations, guest communication, cleaning, and maintenance for their holiday rentals.

Also property management companies may target the owners of student housing facilities such as dormitories or off-campus housing complexes. Student housing operators require specialized property management services to meet the specific demands of student renters, such as lease terms adapted to academic calendars, maintenance services targeted to student lifestyles, and amenities tailored to student preferences. By providing specific services for student housing properties, property management companies may capitalize on the need for student housing while also providing vital support to educational property owners.

Whether they serve individual property owners, real estate investors, commercial property developers, homeowners' associations, or niche markets within the real estate industry, property management companies play an important role in maximizing the value and profitability of real estate properties while providing valuable support to their clients.

Competitive Analysis

The competitive landscape is critical for entrepreneurs trying to launch a property management company. A detailed competition study enables entrepreneurs to discover strengths and weaknesses, analyze market saturation, and uncover areas for difference.

Competitor analysis begins with identifying direct rivals, which are other property management companies that operate in the same geographic region and target similar clients. These rivals might range in size, scope, and service offerings, from huge, established companies to smaller, boutique organizations. Entrepreneurs may learn about their rivals' service offerings, pricing methods, and levels of customer satisfaction by reviewing their websites, marketing materials, and client evaluations.

In addition to direct rivals, entrepreneurs should also consider indirect competitors, which are companies that provide similar services or compete for the same target audience but operate in other industries.

This might include real estate agents, rental listing sites, or DIY property management software vendors.

Understanding the strengths and weaknesses of indirect rivals can help entrepreneurs identify potential threats and opportunities in a larger market environment.

Studying competitors helps in determining their strengths and shortcomings across a variety of dimensions. This involves assessing criteria such as service quality, price, customer service, market reputation, and technical capabilities. Benchmarking against rivals allows businesses to discover areas where they may differentiate themselves and provide distinct value propositions to clients.

As an entrepreneur you should also analyze the hurdles to entry into the property management sector and assess market saturation in their desired geographic location. High entry barriers, such as regulatory restrictions, capital expenditure, and specialized skills, may reduce the number of market competitors while creating chances for new entrants.

In contrast, in a highly saturated market with several rivals, entrepreneurs may need to explore niche markets or develop distinct service offers in order to stand out. You have to monitor industry trends and changes to stay ahead of emerging competitors and market shifts. This entails keeping up with new entrants, technology improvements, legislative changes, and adjustments in customer tastes.

Entrepreneurs may anticipate changes in the competitive landscape and adjust their plans accordingly to preserve a competitive advantage by remaining watchful and adaptive.

Legal and Regulatory Landscape

Entrepreneurs who want to launch a property management firm must understand the legal and regulatory landscape. Property management entails addressing a wide range of legal and regulatory concerns, such as landlord-tenant rules, fair housing regulations, property upkeep standards, and licensing requirements.

Landlord-tenant laws are an important part of the legal landscape because they govern the rights and duties of landlords and tenants in rental agreements. These laws vary by state and address topics like lease agreements, rent payments, security deposits, eviction processes, and property upkeep obligations. Entrepreneurs beginning a property management company must be aware of the landlord-tenant regulations in their chosen market in order to comply and prevent legal problems with customers and renters.

You have to understand the fair housing standards ban discrimination in housing based on race, color, religion, national origin, gender, familial status, or handicap.

Property management companies must follow fair housing rules when advertising rental properties, screening tenants, and enforcing lease agreements. This includes performing fair and consistent tenant screenings, making appropriate accommodations for renters with disabilities, and avoiding discriminatory practices throughout the tenant selection and eviction processes. Property management companies must adhere to property maintenance standards and construction rules to ensure the safety and habitability of their rental homes.

This involves conducting regular property inspections, responding to maintenance concerns immediately, and making the required repairs to keep the property in accordance with local building laws and regulations. Failure to meet property upkeep requirements can result in fines, penalties, and legal ramifications for property management companies.

Licensing requirements differ by state and might include real estate broker licenses, property management licenses, or business licenses. Entrepreneurs starting a property management company must understand the licensing requirements in their chosen market and secure any necessary licenses or certificates to legally run their firm. This may include attending pre-licensing education classes, passing licensing examinations, and submitting license applications to the appropriate regulatory bodies.

As a property management company entrepreneur, you must adhere to financial regulations and accounting standards when managing client cash and keeping financial records. This includes setting up trust accounts for security deposits and rental payments, keeping correct financial records, and complying with generally accepted accounting principles (GAAP) and financial reporting standards.

Finally, property management companies must stay current on changes in the legal and regulatory landscape that may affect their operations. This involves keeping track of changes to landlord-tenant legislation, fair housing standards, construction codes, licensing requirements, and other applicable regulations. Property management companies may assure compliance and reduce legal risks by remaining up-to-date on legal advancements and regulatory changes.

Legal Frameworks for Maintaining Compliance

When launching a property management firm, entrepreneurs must traverse a complicated web of rules, regulations, and policies that control various elements of the real estate market. These legal frameworks are vital for maintaining compliance, preserving the interests of customers and renters, and reducing legal risks.

Let's look at some significant topics in property management law, legislation, and policy:

1. **Landlord-Tenant Laws:** Landlord-tenant laws define landlords' and renters' rights and obligations under rental agreements. These regulations address a wide range of concerns, including lease agreements, rent payments, security deposits, eviction processes, and property maintenance obligations. To avoid legal conflicts and ensure seamless landlord-tenant interactions, property management organizations must understand and

comply with landlord-tenant legislation to avoid legal conflicts and guarantee seamless landlord-tenant interactions.

2. **Fair Housing Laws**: Fair housing laws prohibit discrimination in housing on the grounds of race, color, religion, national origin, sex, familial status, or handicap. Property management companies must follow fair housing rules when advertising rental units, screening renters, and enforcing lease agreements. This involves performing fair and consistent tenant screenings and offering appropriate accommodations for renters with impairments.

3. **Property Maintenance Standards**: Property management organizations are responsible for keeping rental properties in conformity with local building codes and property maintenance standards. This involves conducting regular property inspections, addressing maintenance concerns immediately, and making the required repairs to

guarantee the safety and habitability of rental units. Failure to comply with property upkeep requirements can result in fines, penalties, and legal consequences.

4. **Licensing Requirements:** Many states need property managers to get particular licenses or certificates to lawfully conduct their firms. Licensing requirements may vary based on the state and the type of services provided by the property management firm. To ensure compliance with regulatory authorities, entrepreneurs starting a property management firm must understand the licensing requirements in their chosen market and secure any necessary licenses or certificates.

5. **Financial rules:** Property management organizations must comply with financial rules and accounting standards while managing client cash and maintaining financial records. This includes creating trust accounts for security deposits and rental payments, keeping correct financial records,

and following generally accepted accounting principles (GAAP) and financial reporting standards.

6. **Local Zoning and Land Use Rules:** Local zoning and land use rules control how properties can be utilized and developed within certain geographic areas. Property management organizations must understand local zoning ordinances and land use restrictions to ensure rental properties comply with applicable zoning laws. This may include limits on land use, building heights, parking requirements, and signage laws.

7. **Taxation rules**: Property management organizations must comply with taxation rules pertaining to real estate transactions, rental revenue, and company taxes. This includes knowing the tax deductions and credits available to property owners, properly reporting rental revenue and costs, and complying with federal, state, and local tax rules.

In short, starting a property management firm involves a detailed awareness of the legal and regulatory structure controlling the real estate market.

Conducting a Feasibility Study

Conducting a feasibility study is a critical stage in the process of beginning a property management firm. This comprehensive study examines the viability and possible success of the company concept by considering numerous elements such as market demand, competition, financial predictions, and regulatory issues. Let's go into the components of completing a feasibility study for a property management firm.

This is where market research provides the cornerstone of a feasibility study. Entrepreneurs need to examine the need for property management services in their target market. This entails assessing factors such as population growth, real estate market trends, rental vacancy rates, and the number of rental units in the region. Entrepreneurs analyzing the characteristics of the local real estate market, entrepreneurs may measure the demand for property management services and find opportunities for expansion.

Moreover, a feasibility study assesses the competitive landscape within the property management business. Entrepreneurs need to examine existing property management firms operating in their target market and analyze their strengths, shortcomings, service offerings, pricing tactics, and market positioning. This competitive study helps entrepreneurs find gaps in the market and possibilities to differentiate their firm from rivals.

It also helps with financial predictions are another crucial part of a feasibility study. Entrepreneurs need to examine the financial viability of beginning a property management firm by estimating income, costs, and profitability. This includes determining start-up costs such as office space, equipment, marketing expenses, and licensing fees, as well as ongoing expenses such as payroll, rent collection, maintenance charges, and utilities.

Furthermore, performing a feasibility study entails examining the regulatory environment and legal requirements related to beginning a property management firm. Entrepreneurs need to investigate licensing requirements, zoning rules, landlord-tenant legislation, fair housing standards, and other legal factors that may affect the running of the business. By knowing the regulatory landscape, entrepreneurs may ensure compliance with laws and regulations and reduce legal risks.

Additionally, a feasibility study investigates the operational elements of starting a property management firm. Entrepreneurs need to analyze operational requirements such as workforce demands, technology requirements, property management software, and administrative processes. By determining the resources and infrastructure needed to operate the firm successfully, entrepreneurs may design a realistic plan for establishing and operating the business.

Performing a feasibility study entails identifying potential risks and obstacles that may affect the profitability of the property management firm. This entails detecting external variables such as economic conditions, market fluctuations, legislative changes, and unanticipated occurrences such as natural catastrophes or public health emergencies.

By doing a thorough risk analysis, entrepreneurs may establish methods to manage risks and maintain the resilience of the firm.

In essence, doing a feasibility study is vital for entrepreneurs intending to launch a property management firm. By considering market demand, competition, financial forecasts, regulatory concerns, operational needs, and potential dangers, entrepreneurs may assess the feasibility and potential success of the company concept.

A well-executed feasibility study delivers useful insights that drive strategic decision-making and help entrepreneurs create the framework for a successful property management firm.

Assessing Personal and Financial Readiness

Assessing personal and financial preparation is a vital stage for anyone contemplating launching a property management firm. Analyzing both personal traits and financial aspects determines if one is prepared to handle the responsibilities and challenges of entrepreneurship in property management.

Let's examine personal preparation.

Entrepreneurship involves a specific set of human traits and talents, including leadership, communication, problem-solving, decision-making, and resilience. Property management requires working with customers, renters, contractors, and other stakeholders on a daily basis, so excellent interpersonal skills and the ability to create and maintain relationships are necessary. Additionally, property management typically entails addressing complicated issues and resolving disagreements, so good problem-solving and decision-making abilities are necessary.

Entrepreneurs must also be tough and adaptive, as they may meet problems and failures along the way.

You as an entrepreneur must assess your level of industry knowledge and property administration skills. While formal education and training in real estate or property management can be advantageous, practical experience and understanding of local market dynamics are equally crucial. Entrepreneurs should review their understanding of landlord-tenant legislation, fair housing rules, property maintenance standards, and other legal and regulatory criteria that govern the property management sector in their target market.

Moreover, establishing financial preparedness is vital for entrepreneurs contemplating beginning a property management firm. Property management includes start-up costs such as office space, equipment, licensing fees, and marketing charges, as well as operations costs such as payroll, rent collection, maintenance costs, and utilities.

Entrepreneurs need to analyze their financial resources and determine if they have enough money to cover these charges and continue the firm until it becomes profitable.

Additionally, entrepreneurs need to examine their risk tolerance and desire to commit time, effort, and money to creating and expanding a property management firm. Entrepreneurship takes passion, patience, and a willingness to take calculated risks. Entrepreneurs should analyze their dedication to the business endeavor and their willingness to devote the time and effort necessary to achieve success in the competitive property management market.

The need of a support system cannot be swept under the carpet, there is need to analyze your support system and the resources accessible to you as an entrepreneur. This includes assessing your access to professional networks, mentors, advisers, and other resources that can provide direction, support, and assistance in starting and operating a property management firm. Having a solid support system may be important for entrepreneurs navigating the hurdles of entrepreneurship and developing successful firms.

Identifying Potential Risks and Challenges

Starting a property management firm comes with its share of possible risks and problems that entrepreneurs must recognize and handle to ensure the success and sustainability of their operation. These risks and difficulties involve numerous facets of the firm, including operational, financial, legal, and competitive considerations.

It is obvious that the biggest hazards of launching a property management firm is the possibility of financial instability. Entrepreneurs must carefully analyze the financial viability of their company concept, including start-up costs, operational expenditures, and revenue expectations. Insufficient capital or improper financial planning can lead to cash flow challenges, making it difficult to meet expenses such as office space, equipment, employment, marketing, and ongoing operating costs.

Moreover, economic downturns or volatility in the real estate market can damage demand for property management services and harm the financial health of the organization.

Legal and regulatory compliance is another big risk. Property management organizations must conform to a wide range of laws, regulations, and industry standards covering areas such as landlord-tenant interactions, fair housing policies, property maintenance standards, licensing requirements, and financial controls. Failure to comply with these legal and regulatory standards can result in fines, penalties, litigation, harm to reputation, and even the loss of company licenses. Additionally, developing regulatory changes or new laws can pose issues for property management organizations, which need continual monitoring and adaptation to be compliant.

Operational issues also abound in the property management business. Staffing challenges may include finding and maintaining skilled property managers, leasing agents, maintenance specialists, and administrative staff.

Recruiting and keeping qualified personnel may be tough, particularly in competitive employment markets or during periods of significant employee turnover. Additionally, managing several properties and handling maintenance concerns, tenant complaints, and emergencies demand good time management, communication, and organizational abilities.

Property management organizations face the risk of reputational harm and unfavorable criticism from clients, renters, or other stakeholders. Maintaining high standards of professionalism, ethics, and customer service is vital for creating and sustaining a strong reputation in the market. Negative internet reviews, concerns about property care, or disagreements with clients or renters can ruin the firm's reputation and impair its ability to attract new clients and retain existing ones.

The competition in the property management sector is severe, with multiple organizations fighting for clients and market share.

Identifying and separating the firm from rivals, generating distinct value propositions, and successfully marketing services to target clientele are vital for standing out in a competitive environment. Additionally, staying updated on industry trends, technical breakthroughs, and shifting consumer preferences is vital for remaining competitive and adjusting to changing market dynamics.

Financial Projections and Budgeting

When launching a property management firm, having extensive financial estimates and budgeting procedures is vital for ensuring the financial feasibility and longevity of the endeavor. Financial forecasts give insights into the predicted revenues, costs, and profitability of the firm over a set period of time, often the first few years of operation. Budgeting includes allocating financial resources to various expenses and activities, including start-up charges, operational expenses, marketing, staffing, and contingency funds, to guarantee effective use of resources and financial stability.

To begin with, entrepreneurs need to do rigorous market research and analysis to determine the potential demand for property management services in their target area. This involves examining elements such as population demographics, rental vacancy rates, real estate market trends, and the competitive environment to evaluate the size and growth potential of the market. Studying market dynamics, entrepreneurs may build realistic income estimates based on the number of properties handled, average monthly rental prices, and the predicted increase in client base over time.

Entrepreneurs need to assess the start-up costs involved with starting a property management firm. Start-up costs may include expenses like office space, equipment, furniture, property management software, licensing fees, insurance premiums, legal fees, marketing materials, and early working capital. By precisely evaluating start-up expenses, entrepreneurs may establish the amount of cash required to launch the firm and get funding or investment if needed.

Prepare operational budgets to estimate the continuous expenditures associated with running the property management firm. Operating expenses may include employment costs, rent, utilities, property upkeep, repairs, marketing and advertising, professional fees, insurance premiums, taxes, and administrative expenses. Classifying and forecasting operational expenditures, entrepreneurs can set a baseline for financial planning and monitor spending to ensure it corresponds with revenue estimates and profitability objectives.

They need to anticipate income from property management services, which may include leasing fees, management fees, maintenance costs, tenant placement fees, and other ancillary services. Revenue predictions should take into account elements such as pricing strategy, service offerings, market demand, and the competitive environment to generate realistic revenue objectives. By estimating revenues, entrepreneurs can analyze the firm's profitability and make educated decisions regarding pricing, service offers, and resource allocation.

Moreover, financial predictions should incorporate cash flow forecasts to anticipate the timing and quantity of cash inflows and outflows over a certain period of time. Cash flow projections help enterprises anticipate times of positive and negative cash flow, prepare for financing needs, and manage working capital successfully. Businesses may discover possible cash flow gaps and develop methods to overcome them, such as getting funding, improving revenue streams, or reducing costs by analyzing cash flow estimates.

Additionally, entrepreneurs must develop financial performance measures and key performance indicators (KPIs) to track and analyze the property management firm's financial health and success. Financial metrics may include profitability ratios, such as gross profit margin, net profit margin, and return on investment (ROI), as well as liquidity measures, such as the current ratio and quick ratio. By constantly monitoring financial indicators and KPIs, entrepreneurs may review the business's financial performance, find areas for development, and make data-driven choices to enhance profitability and sustainability.

Creating a Business Plan

This is a vital step for entrepreneurs embarking on the road to launching a property management firm. A well-crafted business plan acts as a roadmap that specifies the vision, goals, strategies, and operational structure for the organization. It includes a detailed review of the business model, market analysis, competitive environment, financial forecasts, and operational strategy, helping entrepreneurs define their business concept and attract investors, lenders, and other stakeholders.

A business plan begins with an executive summary, which gives a succinct overview of the important parts of the business plan. The executive summary outlines the business concept, target market, unique value proposition, competitive advantage, financial predictions, and major milestones. It acts as a snapshot of the business plan, catching the reader's attention and delivering a high-level summary of the company's efforts.

Moreover, a business plan provides a full description of the business strategy and value proposition. This section discusses the property management firm's purpose, vision, and fundamental values, as well as the services provided, target market, and unique value proposition. It articulates the value that the firm delivers to customers and renters, stressing the benefits of participating in the property management services offered.

Additionally, a business strategy contains a complete market study that studies the fundamentals of the local real estate market, including population demographics, rental demand, the competitive landscape, market trends, and growth potential. This research gives insights into the size and features of the target market, as well as the opportunities and problems within the sector. Entrepreneurs may design strategies to capitalize on market opportunities and differentiate their firm from rivals by understanding market dynamics.

Having a business strategy analyzes the competitive environment, identifying important rivals in the property management industry and examining their strengths, weaknesses, service offerings, pricing strategies, and market positioning. This competitive study assists entrepreneurs in identifying market gaps and opportunities to differentiate their firm by delivering unique services or value-added features. By studying rivals' methods and positioning, entrepreneurs can design plans to compete effectively and attract clients in a competitive field. In essence, drafting a business plan is vital for entrepreneurs launching a property management firm. A well-crafted business plan provides a path for success, defining the vision, goals, strategies, and operational structure for the organization.

Legal considerations

Legal concerns are critical in all aspects of founding and operating a property management firm. Entrepreneurs entering this area must manage a complicated web of rules, regulations, and legal requirements in order to assure compliance and reduce possible risks. Understanding and resolving legal factors such as landlord-tenant legislation, fair housing standards, licensing requirements, and liability concerns are critical to a property management firm's profitability and sustainability.

Compliance with landlord-tenant legislation is an important legal aspect for property management companies. These laws govern landlords' and rent landlords' and renter in rental agreements, addressing issues such as lease terms, rent collection, security deposits, property upkeep, eviction processes, and tenant rights. Entrepreneurs must be informed of their jurisdiction's landlord-tenant legislation in order to comply and prevent legal problems with customers and renters.

The company must follow fair housing standards, which prohibit discrimination in housing based on race, color, religion, national origin, gender, familial status, or handicap. Fair housing rules govern several areas of the property management process, including advertising, tenant screening, lease agreements, and tenant relations. Entrepreneurs must put in place fair housing policies and practices to assure compliance and prevent discrimination in their property management operations.

Understand that licensing requirements differ by state and might include real estate broker licenses, property management licenses, or business licenses. Entrepreneurs starting a property management company must understand the licensing requirements in their chosen market and secure any necessary licenses or certificates to legally run their firm. Failure to secure the necessary licenses or certificates can lead to fines, penalties, and legal ramifications for the company. And also property management companies must adhere to property maintenance standards and construction rules to ensure the safety and habitability of their rental homes.

This involves conducting regular property inspections, responding to maintenance concerns immediately, and making the required repairs to keep the property in accordance with local building laws and regulations. Failure to meet property upkeep requirements can result in fines, penalties, and legal ramifications for property management companies.

The client cash and financial records must be handle with care in accordance with financial legislation and accounting standards. This includes setting up trust accounts for security deposits and rental payments, keeping correct financial records, and complying with generally accepted accounting principles (GAAP) and financial reporting standards. Entrepreneurs must guarantee that customer funds are handled properly to avoid charges of financial mismanagement or theft.

Property management companies may face legal risks and responsibility issues arising from property damage, personal injury, or other mishaps on rental properties. Entrepreneurs must get enough insurance coverage, such as general liability insurance, professional liability insurance, and property insurance, to safeguard their company from any legal claims and financial damages. Furthermore, applying risk management tactics, including rigorous tenant screening, frequent property inspections, and timely maintenance, may help property management companies reduce legal risks and liabilities.

Staying up-to-date on changes in the legal environment is critical for property management companies to remain compliant and successfully manage legal risks. The legal landscape surrounding property management is dynamic and always changing, with revisions to landlord-tenant legislation, fair housing standards, licensing requirements, and financial controls.

Legislative changes at the municipal, state, or federal levels, for example, may impose new laws or regulations that have an impact on property management methods. These improvements might include modifications to eviction processes, rent control legislation, anti-discrimination policies, and rental property safety and habitability requirements. To guarantee compliance and avoid legal liability, property management companies must remain up to speed on these developments and adjust their policies, processes, and practices as needed.

In addition, court rulings and legal precedents can have an impact on property management practices and legal requirements. Landlord-tenant conflicts, fair housing complaints, and other legal proceedings may result in court decisions that affect property management companies' rights and obligations. Monitoring legal changes and being current on important case law may help property management companies understand their legal duties and modify their methods to reduce legal risks.

Property management companies must constantly monitor and react to changes in the legal environment in order to assure compliance and successfully limit legal risks. Property management companies that stay up-to-date on legislative updates, court decisions, regulatory actions, and industry trends can proactively address legal issues, uphold ethical standards, and lay the groundwork for long-term success in the dynamic and changing property management industry.

Business Structure

Choosing the correct business structure is an important decision for entrepreneurs beginning a property management company since it affects several areas of the firm, such as liability, taxation, ownership, and operational flexibility. There are numerous business structures to consider, each having advantages and drawbacks based on personal responsibilities, tax preferences, and long-term corporate objectives.

Sole proprietorship is a frequent business form for property management organization. A sole proprietorship is the simplest and easiest form of business ownership because a single person owns and runs the company. Sole owners have complete control over their firm and its operations, and they record all business revenue and expenses on their personal tax returns. However, sole owners are individually accountable for the business's debts and responsibilities, which puts their personal assets at risk in the case of legal claims or financial liabilities.

Another option for property management companies is a partnership, in which two or more people share ownership and management duties. Partnerships can be either general partnerships, in which all partners share equally in the business's earnings and liabilities, or limited partnerships, in which one or more partners have limited responsibility and are not involved in the day-to-day operations. Partnerships provide flexibility in management and decision-making by allowing partners to pool resources and skills. However, partners are individually accountable for the company's debts and commitments, and conflicts between partners have the potential to interrupt operations and damage relationships.

Property management companies can also operate as limited liability companies (LLCs), which combine the liability protection of a corporation with Members in an LLC benefit from limited liability protection, which shields their personal assets from corporate debts and liabilities. LLCs provide flexibility in management structure and taxes by allowing members to select whether the business is taxed as a pass-through organization or a corporation. Furthermore, LLCs are comparatively straightforward to establish and operate, with fewer strict regulatory requirements than corporations.

Corporations are another business structure option for property management firms, providing the maximum level of liability protection to owners. A corporation is a separate legal entity from its owners, known as shareholders, who are not personally accountable for the company's debts and responsibilities. Corporations have a formal management structure that includes shareholders, directors, and officers. They must also comply with legislative obligations such as submitting articles of incorporation, having shareholder meetings, and keeping corporate documents. Corporations face double taxation, which means profits are taxed at both the corporate and individual levels when delivered to shareholders as dividends.

Finally, property management companies might consider creating a real estate investment trust (REIT), which is a type of organization that owns and manages income-producing real estate properties. REITs must pay at least 90% of their taxable revenue to shareholders in the form of dividends, and they provide tax benefits such as pass-through taxation and exemption from corporate income taxes. REITs must comply with various regulatory criteria, such as asset and income tests, as well as laws governing asset composition and income distribution.

Sole proprietorship.

A sole proprietorship is one of the most basic and easy business forms that entrepreneurs can pick when beginning a property management company. A sole proprietorship is a business owned and run by a single person, known as the sole proprietor. This type of corporate ownership is distinguished by its simplicity, flexibility, and ease of implementation, making it an appealing choice for many small business owners, especially property managers.

One of the main advantages of a single proprietorship is its ease of creation and operation. Unlike other company formations, such as partnerships or corporations, establishing a single proprietorship requires minimum formality and regulatory compliance. In most cases, sole proprietors can begin operating their business under their own name or a fictitious business name, also known as a "doing business as" (DBA) name, without having to register with state or local authorities. This simplified approach enables entrepreneurs to start their property management firm fast and easily, allowing them to focus on client acquisition and property management.

Single proprietors have complete control over the operation and decision-making of their property management company. As the sole owner, the proprietor has complete control over all business decisions, from pricing and service offerings to hiring employees and overseeing day-to-day operations. This degree of autonomy enables sole proprietors to align their firm with their vision, goals, and values without the need to speak with partners or stockholders.

A sole proprietorship has the added benefit of tax flexibility. Sole proprietorships are classified as pass-through entities under the tax code, which means that business profits and losses are reported on the sole proprietor's personal income tax return. This makes tax filing easier and eliminates the need for separate business tax returns, lowering the administrative burden and compliance costs for sole proprietors. Furthermore, sole proprietors may be eligible for certain tax breaks and credits, which can help reduce their taxable income and overall tax liability.

They retain complete ownership and control over the profits generated by their property management business. Unlike partnerships or corporations, where profits are shared by multiple owners or shareholders, sole proprietors retain complete ownership of the business profits. This enables sole proprietors to directly benefit from the success and profitability of their property management business, creating a clear incentive for entrepreneurial effort and innovation.

However, entrepreneurs should be aware that sole proprietorships have limitations and drawbacks. One of the most significant disadvantages is the sole proprietor's unlimited personal liability for the business's debts and obligations. In a sole proprietorship, the business and the owner are considered the same legal entity, so the sole proprietor is personally liable for any debts, lawsuits, or liabilities incurred by the company.

This means that personal assets, such as savings, investments, and real estate, are at risk if the property management company faces legal action or suffers financial losses.

Also, sole proprietors may encounter difficulties in obtaining capital and financing for their property management business. Because sole proprietors usually rely on personal funds, loans, or credit to fund their businesses, they may have limited access to external financing sources such as bank loans or venture capital. This can limit the growth and expansion opportunities for sole proprietorship property management companies, especially in competitive markets or during times of economic uncertainty.

Limited Liability Companies (LLC)

The Limited Liability Company (LLC) is a popular and flexible business structure that provides numerous benefits to entrepreneurs starting a property management company. An LLC combines the limited liability protection of a corporation with the flexible taxation options of a partnership or sole proprietorship, making it a popular choice among small business owners, including property managers.

One of the primary benefits of an LLC is limited liability protection, which protects the personal assets of the company's owners, known as members, from business debts and liabilities. In most cases, LLC members are not personally liable for the company's debts, obligations, or legal claims. This means that in the event of a lawsuit, creditor claim, or financial loss incurred by the property management company, members' personal assets, such as savings, investments, and real estate, are generally protected from seizure or liquidation to meet business obligations.

An LLC provides tax flexibility, allowing members to determine how the business is taxed based on their preferences and financial goals. By default, an LLC is treated as a pass-through entity for tax purposes, which means that business profits and losses are reported on the members' individual tax returns.

This prevents members from facing double taxation, which occurs when profits are taxed at both the corporate and individual levels, as is the case in traditional corporations. Members can also choose to be taxed as corporations by filing Form 8832 with the Internal Revenue Service (IRS), which may be advantageous in certain situations.

LLC offers flexibility in management structure and decision-making, allowing members to direct how the company is managed and operated. An LLC can be managed by either its members (member-managed LLCs) or by appointed managers (manager-managed LLCs). This adaptability enables property management companies to customize their management structure to meet their specific needs and preferences, whether they prefer a hands-on approach with direct participation from all members or a more centralized management structure with designated managers overseeing day-to-day operations.

However, forming an LLC is relatively simple when compared to other business structures, such as corporations. Entrepreneurs can form an LLC by submitting articles of organization to the appropriate state agency and paying the necessary filing fees. The articles of organization usually contain basic information about the LLC, such as its name, address, purpose, management structure, and registered agent. After the articles of organization are filed and approved, the LLC is officially recognized as a legal entity distinct from its owners.

Also, LLCs provide flexibility in ownership and membership, allowing multiple members to participate in the business at varying levels of ownership and involvement. Members can be individuals, corporations, partnerships, or other limited liability companies, and ownership interests can be easily transferred or assigned to new members via buy-sell agreements or operating agreements.

This flexibility in ownership structure enables property management companies to accommodate ownership changes, attract new investors or partners, and facilitate business growth and expansion.

It is important to note that LLCs have some limitations and considerations that entrepreneurs should be aware of before starting a property management company. LLCs, for example, must file annually and have ongoing administrative responsibilities such as holding annual meetings, keeping corporate records, and meeting state reporting requirements. Furthermore, some states levy annual fees or taxes on LLCs, which differ depending on the state of formation.

Corporation

A corporation is a legal entity that exists separately from its shareholders. It is one of the most common and well-known business structures, with numerous benefits for entrepreneurs starting a property management business.

One of the primary benefits of a corporation is the limited liability protection it offers its shareholders. In most corporations, shareholders are not personally liable for the company's debts, obligations, or legal claims. This means that shareholders' personal assets, such as savings, investments, and real estate, are generally protected from seizure or liquidation to pay off business debts or legal obligations. Limited liability protection is especially important for property management companies, which may face risks and liabilities arising from property damage, personal injury, or other accidents on rental properties.

A corporation provides perpetual existence, which means that the company will continue to exist even if its ownership or management changes. Unlike other business structures, such as sole proprietorships or partnerships, which may dissolve upon the death or departure of the owner(s), a corporation can continue to operate indefinitely, providing stability and continuity to the property management industry. This ensures that the company's relationships with clients, tenants, vendors, and other stakeholders are sustainable in the long run.

Also, Corporation provides flexibility in its management structure, with a formal hierarchy of governance made up of shareholders, directors, and officers. Shareholders are the corporation's owners and have the right to vote to elect the board of directors, who are in charge of overseeing the company's management and strategy. The board of directors appoints officers, including the president, CEO, CFO, and other executives, who are in charge of the corporation's day-to-day operations and decision-making. This formal management structure establishes clear roles and responsibilities for corporate governance and accountability to shareholders.

It is important to note that corporations have some limitations and considerations that entrepreneurs should be aware of when launching a property management company. Corporations, for example, face more complex regulatory and administrative requirements than sole proprietorships or partnerships. This includes submitting articles of incorporation, holding shareholder meetings, keeping corporate records, and following state reporting requirements. Furthermore, corporations face double taxation, which means profits are taxed at both the corporate and individual levels when distributed to shareholders as dividends.

Licenses and Permits

Obtaining the necessary licenses and permits is an important step in starting a property management business. Licenses and permits ensure that businesses operate legally and in accordance with local, state, and federal regulations. While the specific requirements may differ depending on the location and nature of the property management services provided, there are a few common licenses and permits that property managers must obtain.

It all depends on the jurisdiction, property management companies may require a real estate broker's or a property management license. These licenses, which are typically issued by state real estate commissions or licensing boards, are required for individuals or businesses that lease, rent, or manage real estate properties on behalf of third parties. To obtain a real estate broker's or property management license, individuals may need to meet certain education and experience requirements, pass a licensing exam, and pay an application fee.

In addition to real estate licensing, property management businesses may be required to obtain local business licenses and permits. These licenses and permits are issued by city or county governments and may differ depending on the location of the business and the services provided. General business licenses, home occupation permits, zoning permits, and occupancy permits are examples of local business licenses and permits commonly used by property management businesses. Entrepreneurs should research their area's licensing requirements and obtain any permits required to legally operate their property management business.

These companies may need to obtain specialized licenses or permits for specific services or activities. For example, if the company provides property maintenance or repair services, it may be required to obtain a contractor's license or trade-specific licenses, such as plumbing, electrical, or HVAC licenses, depending on the type of work done. Similarly, if the company handles tenant security deposits or rental escrow funds, it may require a separate license or permit to keep and manage these funds in accordance with state or local regulations.

Additionally, property management companies should be aware of any federal regulations that may apply to their operations and obtain any necessary permits or certifications to ensure compliance. For example, if the company handles personal or financial information from tenants or property owners, it may be required to follow federal privacy regulations such as the Gramm-Leach-Bliley Act (GLBA) or the Health Insurance Portability and Accountability Act (HIPAA). Similarly, if the business conducts background checks on tenants or employees, it may be required to follow federal fair credit reporting laws, such as the Fair Credit Reporting Act (FCRA).

Insurance Requirements

Insurance is an important part of starting a property management business because it protects against the various risks and liabilities that come with managing real estate properties. Understanding insurance requirements and obtaining adequate coverage is critical for mitigating potential financial losses and protecting the company, its assets, and its stakeholders.

General liability insurance is one of the most important types of insurance for property management businesses. This type of insurance covers third-party bodily injury, property damage, and personal injury claims that may occur during business operations. For example, if a tenant or visitor is injured on a business-managed property, general liability insurance can pay for medical bills, legal fees, and other claim-related expenses.

Furthermore, general liability insurance can protect against property damage caused by the company's operations, such as accidental damage to rental units or common areas.

In addition to general liability insurance, property management companies may require professional liability insurance, also known as errors and omissions (E&O) insurance. Professional liability insurance covers claim of negligence, errors, or omissions in the provision of professional services. For property managers, this could include claims involving poor tenant screening, lease enforcement, maintenance management, or financial management. Professional liability insurance can cover legal defense costs, settlements, or judgments resulting from such claims, providing financial security and peace of mind to the company and its stakeholders.

Furthermore, property management companies should consider purchasing property insurance or commercial property insurance to safeguard the physical assets they manage. Property insurance protects real estate properties and their contents against damage or loss caused by perils such as fire, theft, vandalism, or natural disasters. This type of insurance can help cover the costs of repairing, replacing, or rebuilding damaged properties, allowing the business to recover from unforeseen events and continue operations.

Furthermore, property management companies may be required to obtain landlord insurance or rental property insurance for the properties they own or manage on behalf of clients.

Landlord insurance protects rental properties, including rental units, dwellings, and other structures, from risks such as property damage, liability claims, loss of rental income, and tenant-related issues. This type of insurance is critical for protecting investment property and reducing the financial risks associated with renting out properties to tenants.

Furthermore, property management companies should consider purchasing umbrella or excess liability insurance to provide coverage beyond the limits of their primary insurance policies. Umbrella insurance can provide higher liability limits and more comprehensive coverage for a variety of risks, supplementing general liability, professional liability, and property insurance policies.

This can help protect the company from catastrophic losses or lawsuits that exceed the limits of individual insurance policies, thereby adding an extra layer of financial security.

Furthermore, property management companies may need to consider specialized insurance coverage depending on the properties they manage and the services they provide. For example, if the company manages vacation rental properties, it may require vacation rental insurance or short-term rental insurance to cover the risks associated with short-term rental operations, such as property damage, liability claims, and loss of rental income due to cancellations or property damage.

Contracts and Agreements

Contracts and agreements are critical components of starting and running a property management business because they define the rights, responsibilities, and expectations of the company, its clients, tenants, and other stakeholders. These legal documents protect the interests of all parties involved and provide clarity and certainty in business transactions.

The property management agreement is one of the most widely used contracts in property management. This agreement specifies the terms and conditions of the relationship between the property management company and the property owner or client. It typically includes information about the scope of services provided, the duration of the agreement, the fee structure, and the responsibilities of each party. Property management agreements are critical for setting clear expectations and outlining the roles and responsibilities of both the property manager and the property owner.

Another important contract in property management is the lease agreement, also known as the rental agreement. This contract governs the rental relationship between the property owner and the tenant, outlining the terms and conditions of the rental agreement. Lease agreements typically include the rent amount, lease term, security deposit, pet policy, maintenance responsibilities, and property use rules and regulations. Lease agreements help protect the rights of both landlords and tenants by providing a legal framework for resolving any disputes or issues that may arise during the tenancy.

Property management companies may also enter into contracts with vendors, contractors, and service providers to provide a variety of property maintenance, repair, and improvement services. These contracts specify the scope of work, payment terms, deadlines, and other applicable terms and conditions. Property management companies can ensure that work is completed to the required standards and that both parties understand their rights and obligations by entering into clear agreements with vendors and contractors.

Furthermore, property management companies may be required to enter into agreements with homeowner associations (HOAs) or condominium associations (COAs) if they manage properties in community associations. These agreements define the property management company's and the association's rights and responsibilities, including the scope of services offered, fee structure, governance, and decision-making process. Property management companies can ensure compliance with community rules and regulations by entering into clear agreements with associations, as well as facilitate effective communication and collaboration with association boards and members.

Furthermore, property management firms may need to enter into agreements with insurance companies in order to obtain adequate insurance coverage for their operations. These agreements lay out the terms and conditions of the insurance coverage, such as the types of coverage offered, coverage limits, premium payments, and claims procedures. Property management companies can protect their assets and reduce the financial risks associated with their operations by obtaining comprehensive insurance coverage through contractual agreements.

By establishing clear agreements with professional advisors, property management companies can gain access to the expertise and assistance required to navigate legal and regulatory requirements, mitigate risks, and make informed business decisions.

Setting Up Your Property Management Business

Beginning a property management business is an exciting and rewarding endeavor that demands careful planning, preparation, and execution. Launching and maintaining a property management business requires a number of critical activities, ranging from establishing a solid corporate basis to implementing effective growth and success strategies. Thorough research and market analysis are necessary to understand the local real estate sector, determine target demographics, and assess rivals. This includes analyzing rental property trends, vacancy rates, rental prices, and the need for property management services in your target area. Understanding market trends and consumer wants enables you to successfully tailor your services and marketing strategies to the expectations of property owners and tenants.

Choosing a suitable corporate structure for your property management agency. Common business structures include sole proprietorships, partnerships, limited liability companies (LLCs), and corporations. Each form has benefits and concerns for liability protection, taxes, and management flexibility. It is crucial to consult with legal and financial specialists to determine the best structure for your specific needs and objectives.

Once you've settled on a business structure, you must register your firm and obtain the necessary licenses and approvals to operate legally. This may include registering your company's name, obtaining a real estate broker or property management license, and obtaining local business permits and approvals. Compliance with regulatory requirements guarantees that your property management firm follows the law and maintains trust with customers and stakeholders.

You will also need to write a complete business plan that contains your company's goals, target market, competitive analysis, marketing strategies, financial projections, and operational plans. A well-crafted business plan serves as a road map for your property management company, guiding decision-making and resource allocation. It also provides a framework for measuring progress and analyzing your firm's long-term survival.

In addition to establishing the legal and administrative aspects of your property management firm, you must also develop operational procedures and processes to speed up business operations and deliver high-quality services to clients. This includes developing effective property management practices, implementing robust accounting and reporting systems, and utilizing technology tools and software to automate tasks and boost productivity.

You will also need to build a strong network of industry contacts, including real estate agents, property owners, contractors, vendors, and service providers. Networking and connection development are critical for attracting customers, winning property management contracts, and gaining access to important resources and assistance from the real estate sector. By building solid relationships and maintaining open communication with stakeholders, you can present your property management firm as a trustworthy and trusted industry partner.

Moreover, promoting and advertising your property management firm is critical for attracting new clients and expanding your customer base. This might entail developing a professional website, creating engaging marketing materials, leveraging social media platforms, attending networking events, and running targeted advertising campaigns. Effective marketing strategies increase brand recognition, generate leads, and position your property management firm as a market leader in your area.

Furthermore, providing good customer service and establishing strong client relationships are important to the success of any property management company. This includes promptly responding to consumer inquiries and requests, addressing tenant concerns, and speaking freely with property owners. Providing personalized and attentive service will help you build client trust and loyalty while also separating your property management company from competitors.

Finally, establishing a property management company takes thorough planning, preparation, and execution across several aspects of business operations. Launching and managing a successful property management business entails several key steps, such as conducting market research and selecting a suitable business structure, obtaining licenses and permits, developing a comprehensive business plan, establishing operational systems, developing a network of industry contacts, and implementing effective marketing strategies. By adopting these steps and remaining committed to providing excellent customer service, you can establish your property management firm as a trusted and acknowledged leader in the real estate industry.

Location and Office Setup

Choosing the perfect site and establishing your office are critical components of starting a property management service. Your office's location can affect customer and tenant accessibility, exposure in the local market, and overall operational effectiveness. A well-designed and functional office space may also help to improve your company's professionalism and credibility.

When selecting a location for your property management firm, consider factors such as proximity to your target market, client and tenant accessibility, exposure in high-traffic areas, and rent or lease rate affordability. Ideally, your office should be in a central or easily accessible location so that property owners, tenants, and vendors may visit. This might include choosing a site near major transportation hubs, commercial districts, residential neighborhoods, or other areas with a high concentration of rental properties.

Consider the size and layout of the office space to ensure that it satisfies your company's needs while also creating a comfortable and productive working environment for you and your employees. Determine your space requirements based on the number of employees, the frequency of client meetings and consultations, the need for paperwork and file storage, and the availability of facilities such as parking, bathrooms, and accessibility for people with disabilities.

Furthermore, consider branding and designing your office space to reflect your property management company's knowledge and dependability. This could include creating a modern and inviting welcome area, incorporating your company's logo and branding elements into the decor, and providing a welcoming environment for clients and guests. Invest in high-quality furnishings, equipment, and technology to improve day-to-day operations and efficiency.

In addition to physical office space, consider the technology and infrastructure required to run your property management company. This could include creating a secure network for data storage and communication, purchasing property management software for accounting and client management, and implementing digital marketing tools for client outreach and engagement. By effectively utilizing technology, you can streamline your processes, improve communication with clients and renters, and increase overall business efficiency.

You have to put in to consider the flexibility and adaptability of your office design to accommodate your property management company's future growth and expansion. Consider negotiating flexible lease terms with your landlord, investing in modular furniture and office equipment that can be easily changed or upgraded, and planning for additional space or resources as your business grows.

Consider the significance of creating a healthy and professional work environment in your property management company. This includes encouraging teamwork and collaboration among your employees, providing opportunities for training and professional development, and promoting a positive work-life balance.

Building a friendly and inclusive work environment allows you to recruit and retain top talent while also ensuring the long-term success of your property management company. Selecting a suitable location and establishing your office is an important step in starting a property management company.

Factors such as proximity to your target market, client and tenant accessibility, office layout and architecture, technological infrastructure, future development flexibility, and the establishment of a strong workplace culture should be considered. By carefully planning and organizing your office space, you can create a professional and efficient environment that will help your property management company thrive and succeed.

Equipment and Technology

Equipping your property management company with the right technology and equipment is critical for streamlining operations, increasing efficiency, and providing exceptional service to customers and renters. From property management software to office equipment and communication tools, investing in the right technology can have a significant impact on your company's performance and growth.

Property management software is a valuable tool for managing rental properties, leases, tenants, maintenance requests, financial transactions, and other aspects of property administration. There are several property management software options available, ranging from basic accounting and tenant management systems to full platforms with numerous features and functionalities. When selecting property management software for your company, think about ease of use, scalability, integration with other systems, customer service, and affordability.

Consider investing in customer relationship management (CRM) software to better manage client relationships, track interactions, and communicate with property owners and tenants. CRM software allows you to manage customer contact information, track communication history, plan follow-ups, and handle client inquiries and requests more effectively. CRM software allows you to provide personalized and attentive service to customers while also strengthening relationships.

Using accounting and financial management software to track income and expenses, create budgets, and generate financial reports for your property management company. Accounting software automates processes such as invoicing, bill payment, rent collection, and financial reporting, saving time and reducing the possibility of errors. Seek software solutions specifically designed to meet the needs of property management companies, including customizable reporting, integration with property management software, and support for multiple properties and clients.

Implementing online payment and rent collection technologies to make the rent payment process easier for both renters and property owners. Renters can use online payment platforms to pay their rent, eliminating the need for manual processing and paper checks. These systems also include features like automatic reminders, recurring payments, and online account access, making it easier for renters to manage their rent payments.

In addition to software solutions, purchasing office equipment such as PCs, printers, scanners, and copiers is critical to your property management company's day-to-day operations. Choose dependable and effective equipment that meets your company's needs and increases team productivity. Consider investing in ergonomic furniture and office supplies to create a pleasant and productive working environment for your employees.

And also using communication technologies such as email, phone systems, and messaging apps to improve communication both within your property management company and with clients, renters, vendors, and other stakeholders.

Effective communication is essential for providing excellent customer service, quickly resolving issues, and developing strong relationships with clients and renters. Investing in reliable communication technologies ensures that communication channels are open and accessible to all parties involved in property management operations.

Carefully selecting and installing technology and equipment that meets your company's needs, you can increase productivity, improve customer service, and position your property management firm for long-term success in the real estate industry.

Staff Requirements

Staffing requirements are an important aspect of starting and running a property management firm, as your company's success is heavily reliant on the skills, competence, and dedication of your team members. Depending on the size and complexity of your property management company and the services it offers, you may need to hire property managers, leasing agents, administrative assistants, and maintenance specialists.

The property manager is an important position in any property management company. Property managers are responsible for overseeing daily operations, managing rental properties, dealing with property owners and renters, scheduling maintenance and repairs, handling lease and tenant relations, and ensuring compliance with local rules and laws. Property managers must be able to communicate effectively, pay close attention to detail, solve problems, and grasp property management concepts and practices.

In addition to property managers, personnel requirements may include leasing agents or rental agents, who are responsible for promoting rental properties, presenting them to prospective tenants, screening applicants, negotiating contracts, and assisting with move-in and move-out procedures. To effectively promote and lease homes, leasing agents must have strong interpersonal skills, salesmanship, and knowledge of local rental market trends.

Administrative personnel are critical to a property management company's day-to-day operation. Administrative assistants answer phones, respond to emails, schedule appointments, handle paperwork and documents, process rental applications, and help with accounting and financial management tasks.

Maintenance professionals or workers may be required to perform property maintenance and repairs on rental properties managed by the company. Maintenance technicians are in charge of performing routine maintenance inspections, responding to tenant maintenance requests, scheduling repairs and renovations, and ensuring that properties are well-maintained and meet safety and health standards. Maintenance professionals must have relevant technical knowledge, expertise in property maintenance, and the ability to troubleshoot and resolve issues quickly.

Depending on the size and scope of your property management company, you may need to hire additional staff members, such as accounting professionals, marketing specialists, customer service representatives, or legal consultants, to help with various aspects of your operations. Consider your property management company's specific objectives and goals, as well as the skills and knowledge required to effectively manage your portfolio of properties while providing high-quality services to customers and renters.

When recruiting employees for your property management company, it is critical to choose candidates who share your company's values, culture, and goals. Look for people who are passionate about real estate, customer-oriented, and dedicated to providing exceptional service to both customers and tenants. Conduct thorough interviews, check references, and assess candidates' qualifications, experience, and suitability for positions on your property management team.

Provide regular training and professional development opportunities for your employees to help them improve their skills, knowledge, and performance in their respective professions. Investing in employee training and development not only increases job satisfaction and retention but also ensures that your team members have the skills and knowledge needed to succeed in the property management field.

Establishing professional networks

Developing professional networks is critical to the success and growth of any property management company. Building strong relationships with industry professionals, local businesses, community groups, and other stakeholders can result in new opportunities, valuable resources and support, and increased credibility and reputation in the real estate market.

Real estate agents and brokers comprise one of the most important professional networks for property management companies. Real estate agents play an important role in referring clients to property management firms and vice versa. Partnering with real estate agents, you may gain access to a steady stream of new clients who require property management services for their rental properties. Additionally, working with real estate agents may provide information about local market trends, property listings, and investment opportunities.

Developing relationships with local businesses and service providers can benefit your property management firm in a variety of ways. Contractors, plumbers, electricians, and other maintenance specialists can help you maintain and repair your rental properties on time and consistently. Similarly, collaborating with cleaning companies, landscapers, and other service providers can help you improve the appeal and value of your rental properties, attract high-quality tenants, and increase rental income.

Additionally, connecting with homeowner associations (HOAs), condominium associations (COAs), and property owner organizations can provide excellent networking opportunities for property management firms. Many property owners who serve on association boards may require property management services for rental or investment properties in the area. Networking with organization members, as well as attending group meetings and events, allows you to meet new clients while demonstrating your property management abilities and professionalism.

Attending industry events, conferences, and trade shows is an excellent way to network with other property management professionals, industry experts, and potential clients. These events enable attendees to exchange ideas, share best practices, learn about emerging trends and technology, and make important contacts in the real estate industry.

Using online networking platforms and social media channels allows you to expand your professional network and connect with a larger pool of potential clients and business partners. Joining industry-specific groups and forums on platforms like LinkedIn, participating in online debates, and sharing relevant information can help your property management company establish itself as a thought leader and attract potential clients and collaborators.

Developing Services and Pricing

Creating services and pricing for your property management company is an important step in developing your brand, acquiring clients, and ensuring your operations remain profitable. To effectively develop services and pricing, you must first analyze your target market's wants and preferences, determine your company's unique value proposition, and create service packages that meet the various needs of property owners and tenants.

The first steps in developing services for your property management company is conducting market research to determine the demand for property management services in your target market. This includes researching the local real estate market, assessing competitors, and identifying market gaps or opportunities for your business to capitalize on. Understanding market dynamics and client preferences enables you to tailor your services to the specific needs of property owners and tenants in your area.

Consider your property management company's unique value proposition and how you can differentiate it from competitors. This could include highlighting your experience with specific types of properties (e.g., residential, commercial, vacation rentals), offering specialized services or amenities (e.g., property maintenance, tenant screening, 24-hour emergency response), or providing excellent customer service and support. By clearly defining your services' benefits, you can attract customers who value the quality and dependability of your property management solutions.

Pricing your services requires balancing profitability and market competitiveness. Consider the level of service provided, the size and location of the managed properties, the complexity of management activities, and the current market price for property management services in your area. Depending on the services offered and your clients' preferences, pricing options may include flat fees, percentage-based fees (for example, a percentage of monthly rental income), or a combination of the two.

Put into consideration offering tiered service packages with varying levels of care and pricing to meet the diverse needs and budgets of property owners. For example, you could offer a basic package that includes essential services like rent collection and property maintenance, a standard package with additional services like tenant screening and lease management, and a premium package with comprehensive management services and extra amenities. By offering tiered service packages, you can appeal to a wider range of clients while increasing your earning potential.

In addition to traditional property management services, consider offering value-added services that distinguish your company and benefit your clients. Value-added services may include property marketing and advertising, tenant relocation, property inspection and maintenance reports, financial reporting and analysis, and tenant concierge services. Offering a diverse set of services will help you attract clients who value the convenience and peace of mind that come with comprehensive property management solutions.

Property Maintenance

Property maintenance is an important aspect of property management organizations because it ensures that rental homes are well-maintained, safe, and habitable for tenants while also protecting property owners' investments. Effective property maintenance not only raises the value of rental properties, but it also increases tenant satisfaction, retention, and overall profitability for property management companies.

The management companies are primarily in charge of overseeing routine maintenance activities such as gardening, lawn care, cleaning, and the overall upkeep of rental properties. Regular maintenance prevents minor issues from escalating into major repairs, keeping buildings in good condition and lowering vacancy rates while increasing rental income.

Additionally, property management companies are responsible for planning and supervising repairs and renovations as needed to address maintenance issues or prepare properties for new tenants. This could include restoring plumbing or electrical systems, repairing structural damage, replacing appliances or fixtures, repainting walls, or upgrading facilities to attract high-quality tenants.

When performing maintenance and repairs on rental homes, property management companies must adhere to local construction codes, housing regulations, and safety standards. By staying current on regulatory standards and industry best practices, property management companies can protect tenants' health and safety, avoid costly fines or penalties, and maintain positive relationships with regulatory agencies.

Property management companies must respond quickly to tenant maintenance requests, assess the severity of the issue, and organize immediate repairs or fixes. Furthermore, maintaining open lines of communication with property owners and providing regular updates on maintenance operations fosters trust and transparency in the property management relationship.

Property management companies may choose to outsource specific maintenance tasks to third-party vendors or contractors, such as landscaping companies, cleaning services, plumbers, electricians, and general contractors. Outsourcing maintenance services allows property management companies to access specialized expertise, reduce administrative responsibilities, and ensure quick and correct completion of maintenance tasks.

Technological solutions such as property management software can help property management companies streamline their maintenance operations. Property management software allows businesses to manage maintenance requests, schedule appointments, communicate with tenants and vendors, create work orders, and track maintenance costs. Using technology, property management companies can improve the efficiency, accountability, and transparency of their maintenance operations.

Tenant Screening and Placement

Tenant screening and placement are critical components of property management organizations; they ensure that landlords select dependable tenants who will pay rent on time, maintain the property, and adhere to lease terms. Effective tenant screening and placement methods reduce the risks associated with property management, which include late payments, property damage, and evictions.

The first step in tenant screening is to establish specific screening criteria based on credit history, rental history, income verification, employment status, and criminal background checks. Property management companies can use precise criteria to objectively analyze potential renters and make informed tenant placement decisions.

Property management companies can market rental properties and attract new tenants through various channels, such as online listing platforms, social media, signage, and word-of-mouth referrals, once they establish the screening criteria. To attract qualified candidates, property listings must be clear and informative. This includes details on rental conditions, amenities, rental rates, and application procedures.

Screening potential renters, property management companies should conduct thorough background checks to ensure the accuracy of the information provided by applicants. This may include conducting credit checks to determine applicants' financial responsibility and ability to pay rent, contacting previous landlords to inquire about rental history and behavior, verifying employment status and income to ensure affordability, and conducting criminal background checks to assess potential risks.

These companies should require applicants to complete rental application forms and provide supporting documentation such as pay stubs, bank statements, identification documents, and references. Rental application forms should include questions about job history, rental history, income, and personal references to gather relevant information for the screening process.

Property management companies should assess and evaluate each rental application based on the predetermined screening criteria. This may include assessing applicants' credit scores, rental history, income levels, and background check results to determine their suitability as tenants. Before making a final decision, property management companies should communicate with applicants to address any issues or concerns.

After reviewing applications, property management companies can select qualified candidates and issue rental agreements or leases. The lease agreement should include the terms and conditions of the tenancy, such as the rent amount, lease period, security deposit requirements, maintenance obligations, and other details. Property management companies should ensure that renters understand their rights and responsibilities under the lease agreement and provide clear instructions for signing and executing it.

Property management companies must follow fair housing rules and regulations during the tenant screening and placement process to prevent bias and guarantee equal treatment for all applicants. It is critical to treat all candidates fairly and consistently, regardless of race, color, religion, national origin, gender, familial status, disability, or any other protected characteristic.

Rent Collection.

Rent collection is a critical component of property management organizations since it assures regular cash flow and timely rent payments from renters. Effective rent collection systems help property management organizations maintain financial stability, cover operational expenditures, and provide consistent returns to property owners. To build effective rent collection operations, property management companies must set clear regulations, use technology solutions, and communicate openly with renters.

In order to collect rent, one of the first steps is to include explicit payment terms and procedures in lease agreements or rental contracts. Lease agreements should include the due date for rent payments, acceptable payment methods, late fees or penalties for late payments, and processes for dealing with rent-related concerns. By clarifying these conditions upfront, property management companies may set expectations and minimize misunderstandings with renters about rent payments.

Furthermore, property management companies may expedite rent collection by providing renters with a variety of payment alternatives, including online payments, automatic bank transfers, credit card payments, checks, and money orders. Online rental payment systems and property management software solutions may make rent collection more secure and convenient by allowing renters to pay online from any location at any time. Property management companies have the potential to improve tenant satisfaction and rent payments on time.

In addition to providing clear payment terms and different payment choices, property management companies must properly communicate rent payment deadlines and expectations to renters. This may include giving renters reminders or alerts before the rent due date, providing rent payment instructions and contact information, and swiftly responding to any queries or issues they may have concerning rent payments. Open communication helps to avoid misunderstandings and encourages tenants to make rent payments on schedule.

Additionally, property management companies should establish systematic methods for recording rent payments, monitoring payment status, and following up on late or delayed payments. Property management software can automate rent monitoring and payment reminders, provide rent payment reports, and help you communicate with renters about rent payments. Property management companies may use digital solutions to expedite rent collection operations, decrease administrative expenses, and assure accurate record-keeping.

When tenants fail to pay their rent on time, property management companies must have mechanisms in place to handle late payments and enforce lease restrictions. This may include charging late fines or penalties in accordance with the provisions of the lease agreement, sending official warnings or reminders to tenants regarding missing payments, and commencing legal or eviction processes if required. When dealing with rent-related concerns, property management companies must follow set protocols to safeguard their rights and interests, as well as local landlord-tenant laws and regulations.

Building strong relationships with tenants and providing exceptional customer service may encourage them to prioritize rent payments and openly discuss any rent-related concerns or obstacles they may have. Property management companies should respond to tenants' needs and complaints, handle maintenance issues quickly, and communicate clearly and consistently about rent payment expectations and processes.

Eviction Service

Eviction services are a delicate and legally difficult component of property management firms, generally used as a last resort when tenants fail to comply with lease conditions or pay rent on time. Property management companies must handle the eviction process professionally, ethically, and in accordance with local landlord-tenant laws.

The eviction process typically begins when a tenant fails to pay rent, causes property damage, engages in illegal activity, or violates other lease provisions. To preserve tenants' rights and interests, property management companies must follow specified legal procedures and provide enough notice before commencing eviction proceedings.

This is the first steps to in the eviction process is to send tenants a written notice of lease violation or eviction notice, as required by local landlord-tenant laws. The type of notice and notice period vary according to the reason for the eviction and applicable state or municipal regulations. Eviction notices should clearly state the reason for the eviction, the date by which the tenant must vacate the property, and any steps the tenant can take to avoid eviction.

After serving the eviction notice, property management companies may try to resolve the situation with the tenant through negotiation, mediation, or alternative dispute resolution methods. This could include discussing the lease violation with the tenant, offering payment plans or lease modifications, or responding to any concerns or grievances the tenant may have. In some cases, resolving the issue amicably can prevent formal eviction proceedings and preserve the landlord-tenant relationship.

If attempts to resolve the issue with the tenant prove unsuccessful, property management companies may file an eviction lawsuit in the appropriate court. Eviction lawsuits, also known as unlawful detainer actions, are legal proceedings used to regain possession of the rental property and remove the tenant. When filing eviction lawsuits, property management companies must follow strict legal requirements, such as providing proper notice to the tenant, filing the lawsuit in the appropriate jurisdiction, and adhering to the court's procedural rules and timelines.

When facing an eviction lawsuit, property management companies must attend court hearings, present evidence to support their case, and follow court orders and judgments. This may include gathering documentation to support the eviction claim, such as lease agreements, rental payment records, and evidence of lease violations. Property management companies should also be prepared to respond to any defenses or counterclaims raised by tenants, as well as collaborate with legal counsel to effectively navigate the legal process.

If the court grants an eviction judgment in favor of the landlord, property management companies can obtain a writ of possession from the court, allowing the sheriff or constable to remove the tenant from the property. The sheriff or constable will then set a date to execute the eviction, during which the tenant must vacate the property and the landlord can reclaim possession.

Throughout the eviction process, property management companies must prioritize professionalism, empathy, and respect for tenant rights. Eviction is a serious and consequential action that can result in significant consequences for tenants, such as displacement and homelessness. Property management companies should strive to communicate openly and transparently with tenants, provide resources and assistance in transitioning tenants out of the property, and seek alternatives to eviction whenever possible.

Eviction services are a necessary but sensitive aspect of property management businesses, necessitating strict adherence to legal procedures and ethical standards. Property management companies can navigate the eviction process responsibly and minimize the impact on both tenants and landlords by adhering to proper eviction protocols, communicating effectively with tenants, and prioritizing professionalism and empathy.

Other Value-Added Services

Property management companies, in addition to core property management services such as tenant screening, rent collection, and property maintenance, can offer a variety of value-added services to diversify their offerings, differentiate themselves from competitors, and meet the changing needs of property owners and tenants. These value-added services go beyond traditional property management functions, providing clients with greater convenience, peace of mind, and value.

Property marketing and advertising are two of the value-added services that property management companies can provide. Effective marketing strategies can help property management companies attract prospective tenants, fill vacancies quickly, and increase rental income for property owners. Property management companies can use a variety of marketing channels to showcase rental properties and reach potential tenants, including online listing platforms, social media, email marketing, and targeted advertising campaigns.

The property management company can provide property owners with inspection and maintenance reporting services. Regular property inspections help to identify maintenance issues, safety hazards, and potential risks early on, allowing property owners to address them quickly and avoid costly repairs or damages. Property management companies can provide detailed inspection reports, complete with photographs and recommendations for repairs or maintenance, to keep property owners informed and involved in property upkeep.

Property management companies offer financial reporting and analysis as a value-added service. Property management companies can provide comprehensive financial reports to property owners, such as income statements, expense reports, rent roll summaries, and cash flow projections. Property management companies assist property owners in making informed investment decisions and improving their financial performance.

Additionally, property management companies can provide tenant relocation services to help tenants move in and out of rental properties. Tenant relocation services may include coordinating moving logistics, assisting with packing and unpacking, arranging transportation, and providing information or recommendations for local amenities and services. Property management companies that provide tenant relocation services can help tenants save time and improve their overall experience.

Property management companies can offer tenants concierge services to improve their living experience and differentiate their rental properties. Concierge services may include arranging housekeeping or cleaning services, scheduling maintenance or repairs, coordinating package deliveries, making local restaurant or entertainment recommendations, and assisting with various personal errands or tasks. Property management companies can increase tenant satisfaction and retention by providing personalized concierge services.

They can provide value-added services such as sustainability and energy efficiency to appeal to environmentally conscious property owners and tenants. These services may include conducting energy audits, putting in place energy-saving measures like LED lighting or smart thermostats, installing renewable energy systems like solar panels, and providing resources or incentives for sustainable living. By promoting sustainability initiatives, property management companies can lower operating costs, attract environmentally conscious tenants, and contribute to environmental conservation.

Pricing Strategy

Effective pricing strategies determine the revenue generated by managing properties on behalf of owners. Effective pricing strategies not only ensure business profitability but also help to attract customers and stay competitive in the market. Property management companies must carefully consider a variety of factors when developing pricing strategies in order to strike a balance between profitability and market competitiveness.

Property management companies commonly use percentage-based fee structures as a pricing strategy. The model calculates property management fees based on a percentage of the monthly rental income from each managed property. The percentage of rental income typically ranges from 8% to 12%, but it can vary depending on factors such as the property's location, type, and size, as well as the range of services offered by the property management company. This pricing strategy aligns the interests of property management companies and property owners by increasing the fee with higher rental income, incentivizing the company to maximize rental income and property performance.

Property management companies utilize the flat-fee or fixed-rate pricing model as another pricing strategy. Property management fees are charged at a fixed rate per property, regardless of the rental income generated. Property management companies typically charge flat fees on a monthly or annual basis, which can vary based on the size, type, and location of the property, as well as the scope of services offered. Property owners benefit from predictability and simplicity, knowing the exact amount they will be charged each month or year, regardless of fluctuations in rental revenue.

These companies may provide tiered pricing structures to meet the needs and budgets of various clients. Tiered pricing entails providing multiple service packages or levels of service at varying price points, allowing property owners to select the package that best meets their requirements and budget. For example, property management companies may provide basic, standard, and premium service packages with varying levels of service and pricing tiers. Tiered pricing enables property management companies to serve a wider range of clients and capture market segments with diverse preferences and needs.

In addition, property management companies may use value-based pricing strategies in their pricing models. Value-based pricing involves charging for services based on the perceived value they provide to customers rather than the cost of providing the service. Property management firms can justify higher fees by emphasizing the quality of service, expertise, industry reputation, and added value they offer to property owners. Property management companies can justify premium pricing and differentiate themselves from competitors by focusing on their services' value proposition and benefits.

Also, property management companies may charge for additional services or add-ons in order to generate more revenue streams. These ancillary services could include property marketing and advertising, tenant screening, eviction services, property maintenance and repairs, financial reporting and analysis, and concierge services. By providing a menu of optional services, property management companies can tailor their offerings to meet the specific needs and preferences of their clients while also capturing additional revenue.

Marketing and branding

Marketing and branding are critical components of establishing a successful property management business. Effective marketing and branding strategies assist property management companies in attracting clients, differentiating themselves from competitors, and building a strong market reputation. Property management companies can effectively communicate their value proposition, attract property owners and tenants, and drive business growth by developing a cohesive marketing strategy and establishing a compelling brand identity.

Identifying and understanding the target audience is an important part of marketing for property management companies. Property management companies have two primary customer segments: property owners and tenants. Understanding the needs, preferences, and pain points of these target audiences is critical for creating targeted marketing messages and tailoring services to their specific requirements. Property management companies must conduct market research to determine their target audience's demographics, psychographics, and behavior patterns, allowing them to create marketing strategies that resonate with their customers.

After identifying the target audience, property management companies can develop a comprehensive marketing strategy to reach and engage prospective clients.

The marketing strategy could include a combination of online and offline marketing tactics, such as digital marketing, social media marketing, content marketing, email marketing, search engine optimization (SEO), pay-per-click (PPC) advertising, direct mail campaigns, networking events, and industry partnerships. Property management companies can increase their market reach and visibility by utilizing a variety of marketing channels and tactics, as well as effectively communicating their brand message to potential clients.

For property management companies, branding is another important aspect of marketing. A strong brand identity enables property management companies to differentiate themselves from competitors while also establishing trust and credibility with customers. Branding consists of several elements, including the company name, logo, tagline, colors, typography, imagery, and messaging. Property management companies must create a consistent brand identity that reflects their values, personalities, and distinct selling points. A well-defined brand identity enables property management companies to establish a memorable and recognizable presence in the market, as well as foster positive client perceptions.

Property management companies should prioritize online presence and reputation management as part of their marketing strategy. In today's digital age, potential clients frequently research property management companies online before making a decision. Property management companies must have a professional and user-friendly website that highlights their services, team members, client testimonials, and case studies.

Furthermore, property management companies should actively manage their online reputation by monitoring and responding to client reviews and feedback via review platforms, social media channels, and online forums. Property management companies can boost their credibility and attract more customers by maintaining a positive online presence and responding to client concerns quickly and professionally.

Content marketing is a powerful tool for property management companies to establish thought leadership, educate their target audience, and increase engagement. Property management companies can create and distribute valuable content such as blog posts, articles, whitepapers, e-books, infographics, videos, and podcasts to address common problems, provide solutions, and demonstrate their expertise. By providing valuable and relevant content, property management companies can establish themselves as trusted industry advisors and attract potential clients looking for property management solutions.

Networking and developing relationships with industry stakeholders such as real estate agents, property developers, contractors, and local business associations can help property management companies grow their clientele and generate referrals.

Property management companies can build a strong referral network by attending industry events, joining networking groups, and collaborating with complementary businesses.

Establishing a brand identity

Developing a strong brand identity is critical for establishing a property management company as a credible and trustworthy entity in the market. A well-defined brand identity communicates the company's values, personality, and unique selling proposition to potential customers, distinguishing it from competitors and cultivating positive perceptions among clients and stakeholders.

One of the first steps in developing a brand identity for a property management company is defining its brand purpose and values. The brand purpose expresses the reason for the company's existence beyond profit generation and reflects its mission, vision, and core values. Property management companies should articulate their values, such as integrity, professionalism, transparency, and customer service excellence, to guide their business decisions and client interactions.

Property management companies can create a compelling brand story that connects with their target audience once they establish the brand's purpose and values. The brand story should highlight the company's journey, values, unique selling proposition, and commitment to customer service. Property management companies can differentiate themselves from competitors by telling a compelling brand story that connects with potential clients emotionally.

Creating a memorable and visually appealing brand identity is critical for property management companies seeking to establish a strong visual presence in the market. This includes creating a unique logo, choosing appropriate colors, typography, and imagery, and creating consistent branding elements for all communication channels, such as the website, social media, marketing materials, and signage. The logo is the visual representation of the brand and should be simple, adaptable, and reflective of the company's identity and values.

Additionally, property management companies should carefully consider their brand voice and messaging to ensure consistency and coherence in their client communications. The brand voice refers to the tone, language, and style used in written and spoken communication, such as marketing materials, website content, social media posts, and client interactions. Property management companies should use a brand voice that is consistent with their brand personality and appeals to their target audience, whether it is professional, friendly, authoritative, or empathetic.

Developing a strong brand identity entails creating a comprehensive brand style guide that outlines the guidelines for consistently applying branding elements across all touchpoints. To ensure brand consistency and coherence, the brand style guide should include specifications for logo usage, color palettes, typography, imagery, and brand messaging. By following the brand style guide, property management companies can maintain a consistent and professional brand image while also increasing brand recognition among clients and stakeholders.

Creating a brand identity entails increasing brand awareness and recognition through strategic marketing and branding efforts. Property management companies should use a variety of marketing channels and tactics to increase their visibility and reach with potential clients, such as digital marketing, social media marketing, content marketing, email marketing, and networking events. Property management companies can increase market awareness and recognition by consistently reinforcing their brand identity through these channels.

Developing a strong brand identity is critical for property management companies seeking to establish themselves as reputable and trustworthy market entities. Property management companies can create a cohesive and compelling brand identity that resonates with clients and stakeholders by defining their brand purpose and values, telling a compelling brand story, designing a distinctive visual identity, implementing a consistent brand voice and messaging, developing a comprehensive brand style guide, and leveraging strategic marketing initiatives.

Online Presence

In today's digital age, having a strong online presence is critical to the success of any property management company. An effective online presence not only improves visibility and reach, but it also boosts credibility, fosters trust with potential customers, and propels business growth. Property management companies must use a variety of online platforms and tools to promote their services, engage with clients, and stand out in a competitive market.

A professional and user-friendly website is an important part of developing a property management business's online presence. The website serves as the company's digital storefront and is frequently the first point of contact for prospective customers. Property management companies should invest in developing a well-designed, informative, and user-friendly website that promotes their services, team, client testimonials, and case studies. The website should also have clear calls-to-action (CTAs) that encourage visitors to contact the company, request more information, or schedule a consultation.

Property management companies should optimize their websites for search engines to increase visibility and rank in search engine results pages (SERPs). This entails implementing search engine optimization (SEO) strategies such as keyword research, optimizing on-page elements (e.g., meta tags, headings, and content), producing high-quality and relevant content, obtaining backlinks from reputable websites, and improving website loading speed and mobile responsiveness. Property management companies that optimize their websites for SEO can attract organic traffic from potential clients looking for property management services online.

The property management companies should establish a presence on relevant social media platforms in order to interact with clients and demonstrate their expertise. Social media platforms like Facebook, LinkedIn, Twitter, Instagram, and YouTube enable property management companies to share valuable content, interact with followers, showcase properties, highlight client testimonials, and participate in industry discussions. Property management companies can build a following and improve brand visibility and reputation by posting engaging content on a regular basis, responding to comments and messages, and participating in relevant conversations.

They should make use of email marketing to build relationships with clients and prospects while remaining top-of-mind. Email marketing enables property management companies to send targeted and personalized messages to subscribers, such as newsletters, property updates, industry insights, promotional offers, and event invitations. Property management companies can deliver relevant and valuable content to their clients by segmenting their email lists based on their preferences and interests, which increases engagement and conversions.

Online review platforms and directories play an important role in shaping property management companies' online reputations. Property management companies should actively monitor and manage their online presence on review platforms such as Google My Business, Yelp, and Facebook Reviews, responding to client reviews and feedback in a timely and professional manner. Positive feedback and testimonials from satisfied customers can significantly boost a property management company's credibility and reputation, attracting new clients. In addition, property management companies can use online advertising strategies such as pay-per-click (PPC) advertising, display advertising, and social media advertising to boost visibility and reach specific audiences. PPC advertising enables property management companies to bid on keywords related to their services and place ads prominently in search engine results and on relevant websites. Property management businesses can use social media advertising to target specific demographics, interests, and behaviors and reach out to potential clients.

In today's digital landscape, property management companies must establish a strong online presence in order to attract clients, increase credibility, and drive business growth. By investing in a professional website, optimizing for search engines, engaging on social media, implementing email marketing, managing online reviews, and leveraging online advertising, property management companies can create a compelling online presence that resonates with clients and distinguishes them from the competition.

Traditional Marketing Strategies

Traditional marketing approaches continue to play a significant role in promoting and developing property management businesses, complementing digital marketing efforts, and connecting customers through physical channels. These strategies involve conventional media and methods to boost brand awareness, attract clients, and develop leads in the local market.

One of the most popular conventional marketing strategies for property management services. This entails putting advertisements in local newspapers, magazines, real estate journals, and community newsletters. Print advertising allows property management organizations to target a concentrated local audience, including property owners and investors, who may be seeking property management services. By intentionally choosing newspapers with adequate audience demographics and distribution areas, property management businesses may optimize the efficacy of their print advertising campaigns.

Property management businesses commonly use direct mail marketing as a marketing strategy. Direct mail comprises providing promotional goods such as postcards, flyers, pamphlets, and newsletters directly to specific mailing lists of potential clients. Property management businesses may use direct mail to market their services, demonstrate their expertise, and provide special deals or discounts to attract new clients. Customize direct mail campaigns based on criteria such as area, property type, and client preferences to boost performance and generate leads.

Additionally, property management businesses may leverage classic networking and relationship-building strategies to increase their client base and offer referrals. This entails visiting local networking events, industry conferences, and trade exhibitions to meet with real estate professionals, property owners, investors, and industry stakeholders.

Building personal relationships and developing a strong network of contacts within the local community may lead to referrals and word-of-mouth recommendations, improving company development for property management firms.

Furthermore, property management businesses may employ conventional signage and outdoor advertising to improve awareness and attract new clients in their local market. This entails erecting signs, banners, and billboards in high-traffic sites such as busy streets, commercial districts, and real estate developments to sell their services and generate leads. Effective signage and outdoor advertising should feature clear branding, messaging, and contact information to persuade interested prospects to ask about property management services.

Moreover, property management businesses might participate in community outreach and sponsorship opportunities to build awareness and promote goodwill in the local community. This includes supporting local events, sports teams, charity fundraisers, and community initiatives to boost brand awareness and demonstrate corporate social responsibility. Community participation helps property management firms create a wonderful reputation and strengthen ties with local individuals, businesses, and organizations, leading to prospective client referrals and business chances.

This conventional marketing methods remain crucial tools for property management firms to promote their services, attract clients, and produce leads in the local market. Print advertising, direct mail marketing, networking and relationship-building, signage and outdoor advertising, and community outreach can all help property management companies reach their target audience, increase brand awareness, and drive business growth. While digital marketing has proven increasingly vital in today's digital environment, conventional marketing approaches continue to complement and enhance the complete marketing plan for property management firms.

Networking and partnerships

Networking and creating strategic contacts are key components of launching and building a successful property management business. By proactively communicating with industry stakeholders, developing meaningful connections, and fostering mutually beneficial relationships, property management firms may expand their client base, increase referrals, and position themselves as trusted leaders in the area.

One of the primary networking methods for property management firms is to attend industry events, conferences, and trade fairs. These events provide a wonderful opportunity to interact with real estate professionals, property owners, investors, contractors, vendors, and other industry stakeholders. Property management business owners and representatives may participate in relevant conversations, share contact information, and develop relationships with new clients and reference sources. Attending industry events also enables property management businesses to stay current on industry trends, best practices, and impending possibilities.

Property management businesses may join local networking clubs and groups to expand their professional network and gain awareness of the local market. Joining organizations such as real estate associations, property management associations, business networking groups, and chambers of commerce allows the opportunity to meet like-minded individuals, discuss ideas, and collaborate on commercial opportunities. Property management firm owners may use these networking associations to portray themselves as renowned industry experts and gain recommendations from fellow members.

Additionally, forming strategic alliances with complementary businesses and service providers may increase the value proposition of property management services and broaden the range of services provided to clients. For example, property management firms can unite with real estate agents, brokers, and property developers to provide complete property management solutions to their clients. By partnering with real estate specialists, property management businesses may reach a broader consumer base and develop referrals from clients in need of property management services.

Moreover, property management corporations can develop arrangements with contractors, maintenance providers, cleaning services, landscaping companies, and other vendors to offer value-added services to consumers. Property management firms can ensure the quality and dependability of services offered to consumers, enhance tenant contentment, and differentiate themselves from competitors by partnering with reputable service providers. Building strong relationships with vendors also enables property management businesses to negotiate competitive terms and pricing for services, ultimately improving the bottom line.

Property management businesses may leverage online platforms and social media channels to extend their professional network and connect with industry players beyond their local market. Platforms such as LinkedIn allow property management professionals to join industry groups, participate in conversations, and connect with individuals from across the world. By actively engaging in internet networking, property management businesses may position themselves as thought leaders in the area and build links with potential clients and partners overseas.

Client Testimonials and Reviews

Client testimonials and reviews play a crucial role in the success of a property management service, acting as useful tools for creating reputation, generating trust, and recruiting new clients. These testimonials and reviews provide real-world insights into the quality of service, professionalism, and contentment experienced by previous and current clients, shaping the decision-making process of potential clients considering property management services.

Client testimonials work as vital confirmations of a property management business's offerings, talents, and expertise. A well-crafted testimonial from a satisfied client highlights the positive experiences and outcomes achieved by the partnership with the property management agency. Testimonials often underline vital benefits such as effective communication, responsiveness, attention to detail, and overall contentment with the management of their properties. By displaying these testimonials on their website, marketing materials, and social media channels, property management businesses can leverage the excellent remarks to create credibility and attract new clients.

Internet evaluations on platforms such as Google My Service, Yelp, Facebook, and industry-specific review sites are vital in developing the reputation and perception of a property management business. Potential clients frequently rely on these reviews to determine the level of service, professionalism, and customer satisfaction provided by a property management organization before deciding to hire their services. Positive reviews from satisfied clients serve as valuable endorsements, while negative reviews provide opportunities for property management businesses to address concerns, demonstrate their commitment to client satisfaction, and showcase their responsiveness and professionalism in handling feedback.

In addition to textual testimonials and assessments, property management firms may also deploy video testimonials to further increase their reputation and authenticity. Video testimonials allow satisfied clients to communicate their experiences and satisfaction with the property management services in a more customized and engaging manner. These video testimonials present potential consumers with a glimpse into the amazing experiences and outcomes acquired by clients working with the property management organization, helping to develop trust and confidence in their services. Property management businesses may actively encourage and seek client feedback and evaluations through a variety of channels. This can entail sending follow-up emails or surveys after completing a successful property management project, gathering information from clients during typical interactions, or persuading clients to post reviews by granting discounts or incentives for their participation. By proactively asking for customer comments and evaluations, property management businesses may obtain helpful input, strengthen their brand, and emphasize their devotion to client pleasure and quality in service delivery.

It is vital for property management firms to continually monitor and maintain their internet reputation by replying immediately and professionally to client evaluations and comments, whether favorable or unfavorable.

Acknowledging good reviews and showing appreciation for comments displays respect for clients' support and satisfaction. Similarly, addressing concerns noted in unfavorable reviews with empathy, honesty, and a dedication to resolution may help mitigate any potential damage to the business's reputation and demonstrate their devotion to customer pleasure and ongoing growth.

Customer testimonials and reviews are crucial assets for property management firms, serving as strong endorsements of their services and influencing the decision-making process of potential clients. Showcasing authentic testimonials, actively soliciting client feedback, and effectively managing their online reputation, property management businesses can build credibility, establish trust, and attract new clients, ultimately contributing to their long-term success and growth in the competitive property management industry.

Traditional marketing strategies

Traditional marketing methods continue to play an important role in promoting and expanding property management firms, supplementing digital marketing efforts, and engaging clients via physical channels. These techniques use traditional media and methods to increase brand recognition, attract customers, and generate leads in the local market.

One of the most commonly used conventional marketing tactics for property management services. This includes placing ads in local newspapers, magazines, real estate journals, and community newsletters. Print advertising enables property management companies to target a specific local audience, including property owners and investors who may be looking for property management services. Property management companies may improve the effectiveness of their print advertising efforts by carefully selecting newspapers with appropriate target demographics and distribution zones.

Property management companies frequently employ direct mail marketing as a marketing tactic. Direct mail refers to the distribution of promotional materials such as postcards, brochures, booklets, and newsletters to particular mailing lists of potential clients. Property management companies can use direct mail to sell their services, demonstrate their competence, and provide special deals or discounts to attract new clients. To improve effectiveness and create leads, tailor direct mail campaigns to specific areas, property types, and customer preferences.

Furthermore, property management companies may use traditional networking and relationship-building techniques to grow their customer base and give referrals. This includes attending local networking events, industry conferences, and trade shows to interact with real estate professionals, property owners, investors, and other industry players. Building personal ties and a strong network of contacts in the local community may lead to referrals and word-of-mouth recommendations, which can help property management organizations grow their businesses.

Furthermore, property management companies may use traditional signs and outdoor advertising to raise awareness and recruit new customers in their local market. This comprises putting up signs, banners, and billboards in high-traffic areas, including busy streets, business districts, and real estate developments, to offer their services and create leads. Effective signage and outdoor advertising should have clear branding, messaging, and contact information to entice potential customers to inquire about property management services.

These property management companies may participate in community outreach and sponsorship opportunities to raise awareness and create goodwill in the local community. Supporting local events, sports teams, charity fundraisers, and community activities may help enhance brand exposure and demonstrate corporate social responsibility. Community involvement enables property management services to build a strong reputation and improve links with local people, businesses, and organizations, resulting in potential client referrals and commercial opportunities.

Traditional marketing strategies are still important tools for property management organizations to promote their services, attract clients, and generate leads in the local market. Print advertising, direct mail marketing, networking and connection development, signage and outdoor advertising, and community engagement are all effective ways for property management firms to contact their target audience, raise brand recognition, and promote company growth. While digital marketing has become increasingly important in today's digital world, traditional marketing tactics continue to complement and enrich the overall marketing strategy for property management organizations.

Networking and Partnerships

Networking and making strategic connections are critical components of starting and growing a successful property management firm. Property management businesses may grow their client base, generate referrals, and position themselves as trusted leaders in the region by proactively interacting with industry players, making meaningful connections, and cultivating mutually beneficial partnerships. Attending industry events, conferences, and trade fairs is one of the most effective networking strategies for property management organizations.

These events offer excellent opportunities to network with real estate professionals, property owners, investors, contractors, vendors, and other industry players. Property management firm owners and representatives may engage in pertinent conversations, exchange contact information, and create relationships with new clients and referral sources. Attending industry events also allows property management companies to stay current on industry trends, best practices, and potential opportunities.

Furthermore, property management companies might join local networking clubs and associations to broaden their professional network and acquire insight into the local industry. Joining organizations like real estate associations, property management associations, business networking groups, and chambers of commerce helps you meet others who share your interests, exchange ideas, and cooperate on business prospects.

Property management business owners can utilize these networking groups to position themselves as industry experts and get referrals from other members. Furthermore, building strategic relationships with complementary firms and service providers may improve the value proposition of property management services and widen the variety of services available to clients. For example, property management companies can collaborate with real estate agents, brokers, and developers to provide their clients with comprehensive property management solutions.

Property management companies that collaborate with real estate professionals can reach a larger customer base and generate recommendations from clients in need of property management services. These businesses can form partnerships with contractors, maintenance providers, cleaning services, landscaping firms, and other vendors to deliver value-added services to customers. Partnering with respected service providers allows property management organizations to assure the quality and dependability of services provided to customers, increase tenant satisfaction, and differentiate themselves from competition.

Building excellent ties with vendors also allows property management companies to negotiate competitive terms and pricing for services, which ultimately improves profitability. Property management companies may use internet platforms and social media channels to broaden their professional network and engage with industry participants beyond their local market. Platforms like LinkedIn enable property management professionals to join industry groups, engage in conversations, and connect with people from all over the world. Property management companies that actively engage in online networking may position themselves as thought leaders in the industry and connect with new clients and partners worldwide.

Networking and connections are critical to the success of property management organizations because they allow them to expand their client base, make suggestions, and improve their value proposition. Property management companies can establish a strong professional network, foster meaningful relationships, and position themselves for long-term success in the competitive property management industry by actively participating in industry events, joining networking groups, forming strategic partnerships with complementary businesses, and leveraging online platforms.

Client Testimonials and Reviews

Client testimonials and reviews are critical to the success of a property management firm, serving as effective tools for building reputation, developing trust, and recruiting new clients. These testimonials and reviews give real-world insights into the quality of service, professionalism, and satisfaction of former and present clients, influencing future clients' decision-making processes when selecting property management services. First and foremost, client testimonials serve as important confirmations of a property management company's services, skills, and competence.

A well-crafted testimonial from a delighted customer emphasizes the good experiences and consequences of cooperation with the property management service. Testimonials frequently highlight critical benefits such as good communication, responsiveness, attention to detail, and overall satisfaction with the property management process.

Property management companies may boost their reputation and attract new clients by presenting these testimonials on their website, marketing materials, and social media platforms. Furthermore, online evaluations on platforms such as Google My Service, Yelp, Facebook, and industry-specific review sites are critical in building a property management company's reputation and image.

Potential clients usually depend on these reviews to assess a property management organization's quality of service, professionalism, and customer happiness before hiring them. Positive reviews from satisfied clients are valuable endorsements, whereas negative reviews allow property management companies to address concerns, demonstrate their commitment to client satisfaction, and demonstrate responsiveness and professionalism in dealing with feedback.

In addition to written testimonials and evaluations, property management services may use video testimonials to strengthen their reputation and credibility. Video testimonials enable delighted clients to convey their experiences and pleasure with property management services in a more personalized and engaging format. These video testimonials provide potential customers with a look into the incredible experiences and outcomes obtained by clients working with the property management company, therefore fostering trust and confidence in their services. Furthermore, property management companies may actively encourage and solicit client comments and reviews via a number of means.

This might include sending follow-up emails or surveys following a successful property management project, obtaining information from clients during routine encounters, or getting clients to submit reviews by offering discounts or incentives in exchange for their involvement. By proactively soliciting consumer feedback and assessments, property management companies may gain valuable insights, improve their brand, and stress their commitment to client satisfaction and service quality.

It is critical for property management companies to constantly monitor and maintain their online image by responding quickly and professionally to customer evaluations and comments, whether positive or negative.

Acknowledging positive feedback and expressing gratitude for remarks demonstrates respect for clients' support and happiness. Similarly, responding to issues raised in negative reviews with empathy, honesty, and a commitment to resolution may help offset any possible damage to the company's reputation while also demonstrating their commitment to customer satisfaction and continued growth.

Customer testimonials and reviews are valuable assets for property management organizations since they serve as powerful endorsements of their services and influence future clients' decision-making processes. Property management companies can build credibility, establish trust, and attract new clients by displaying authentic testimonials, actively soliciting client feedback, and effectively managing their online reputation, all of which contribute to their long-term success and growth in the competitive property management market.

Compliance and Risk Management

Compliance and risk management are key parts of running a successful property management firm, as they assure adherence to relevant laws, regulations, and industry standards while limiting possible risks and liabilities. Property managers must negotiate a complicated regulatory framework and proactively manage risks to safeguard their customers, renters, and assets.

One of the important components of compliance and risk management in property management is being aware of the rules and regulations regulating the real estate business. This covers federal, state, and municipal rules pertaining to fair housing, landlord-tenant relationships, property upkeep, environmental restrictions, and more. Property managers must have a solid awareness of these rules and ensure their business activities comply with legal standards to prevent costly penalties, litigation, and reputational harm.

Additionally, property management organizations must create rigorous rules and processes to guarantee compliance with relevant legislation and industry standards. This may include designing and documenting protocols for tenant screening, lease agreements, rent collection, property upkeep, and eviction processes.

Property managers can encourage consistency and responsibility within their business by having clear rules and processes, thereby reducing the risk of non-compliance.

Compliance and risk management entail keeping accurate and up-to-date paperwork related to property management operations. This includes keeping records of lease agreements, rental payments, maintenance requests, property inspections, and contact with renters and property owners. Having extensive documentation not only promotes compliance with legal and regulatory standards, but it also acts as proof in the case of disputes or legal procedures.

Another key part of compliance and risk management is ensuring the safety and habitability of rental buildings. Property managers are responsible for managing buildings in accordance with building codes, health and safety requirements, and other relevant standards. This involves fixing maintenance concerns immediately, conducting regular property inspections, and implementing necessary safety measures to protect tenants and visitors from risks.

Property managers must address potential hazards related to property ownership and management, such as property damage, liability claims, and financial losses. This may entail securing adequate insurance coverage, such as general liability insurance, property insurance, and professional liability insurance, to guard against unanticipated incidents and litigation.

Additionally, property managers should employ risk mitigation tactics, such as completing extensive tenant screens, doing background checks on suppliers and contractors, and implementing preventative maintenance measures to mitigate possible dangers.

In essence, compliance and risk management are critical issues for property management organizations, guaranteeing adherence to legal and regulatory standards while limiting potential risks and liabilities. By staying informed about relevant laws and regulations, establishing clear policies and procedures, maintaining accurate documentation, ensuring property safety and habitability, obtaining appropriate insurance coverage, and implementing risk mitigation strategies, property managers can protect their clients, tenants, and assets while fostering a successful and sustainable business.

Embracing a proactive approach to compliance and risk management is vital for property management organizations aiming to sustain ethical standards, establish confidence with stakeholders, and achieve long-term success in the competitive real estate market.

Fair Housing Laws

Fair housing rules are key standards that property management organizations must comply with when working in the real estate market. These rules are aimed at providing equal access to housing opportunities for all persons, regardless of their race, color, national origin, religion, sex, familial status, or handicap. Understanding and complying with fair housing regulations is vital for property management organizations to avoid discrimination, legal ramifications, and brand harm.

Fair housing laws comprise different federal, state, and municipal acts and regulations that ban discrimination in housing-related activities. Adopted in 1968 as part of the Civil Rights Act, the Fair Housing Act (FHA) is the fundamental federal statute overseeing fair housing practices. It prohibits discrimination based on protected characteristics in the sale, rental, financing, or advertising of residential properties. These protected qualities include race, color, national origin, religion, sex, family status, and handicap.

Property management organizations must educate themselves on the specific regulations of the FHA and guarantee compliance with its obligations.

This includes understanding the prohibitions against discriminatory practices such as refusing to rent or sell housing, setting different terms or conditions for housing transactions, providing different housing services or facilities, or falsely denying the availability of housing based on protected characteristics.

In addition to the FHA, property management organizations must also comply with other federal laws that address fair housing concerns, such as the Americans with Disabilities Act (ADA) and the Housing and Urban Development (HUD) rules. These regulations oblige property managers to offer reasonable accommodations for people with disabilities and ensure accessibility to homes and related facilities.

State and municipal fair housing laws may impose additional obligations and safeguards beyond those granted by federal law. Property management firms operating in various jurisdictions must be aware of and comply with these state and municipal rules to avoid potential legal liability. To guarantee compliance with fair housing legislation, property management organizations should adopt policies and processes that encourage fair and non-discriminatory practices.

This involves developing consistent tenant screening standards, ensuring fair treatment of all applicants and renters, and offering appropriate accommodations for those with disabilities. Moreover, property management personnel should get frequent training on fair housing legislation and best practices to guarantee comprehension and compliance. Training programs should address issues such as fair housing regulations, banned discriminatory behaviors, the management of reasonable accommodation requests, and fostering diversity and inclusion in housing-related activities.

Additionally, property management organizations should keep correct records and paperwork related to housing transactions and tenant contacts in order to comply with fair housing legislation. This includes records of rental applications, lease agreements, interactions with renters, maintenance requests, and any accommodation or modification requests made by persons with disabilities. Fair housing rules serve a critical role in guaranteeing equitable access to housing options and avoiding discrimination in the real estate business.

Property management organizations must understand and comply with federal, state, and municipal fair housing regulations to avoid legal liability and preserve ethical standards. By creating regulations, offering training, and maintaining correct records, property management firms may support fair housing practices and build inclusive housing settings for all people.

Environmental Regulations

Environmental standards are essential concerns for property management organizations as they negotiate the complexity of managing residential and commercial properties. These rules are aimed at preserving the environment and public health by restricting many elements of property development, building, operation, and maintenance.

Property managers must understand and comply with environmental standards to reduce hazards, maintain regulatory compliance, and preserve the well-being of renters, property owners, and neighboring communities.

One of the key environmental requirements that property management organizations must comply with is linked to hazardous chemicals and substances. Properties may include hazardous materials such as lead-based paint, asbestos, mold, radon, or other contaminants that pose health concerns to inhabitants. Property managers are responsible for detecting and resolving these risks in conformity with relevant environmental laws and regulations.

The Environmental Protection Agency (EPA) enforces the Lead-Based Paint Renovation, Repair, and Painting (RRP) Rule, which mandates that property managers take special care when rebuilding or repairing houses built before 1978, potentially containing lead-based paint. Compliance with this requirement entails adequate worker training, safe work procedures, control of lead dust, and disposal of lead-contaminated goods.

Similarly, property managers must remove asbestos-containing materials (ACMs) from buildings, as exposure to asbestos fibers can lead to major health conditions such as lung cancer and mesothelioma. Compliance with asbestos legislation may require completing asbestos surveys, developing management plans, and ensuring the correct removal and disposal of ACMs by registered specialists.

Furthermore, property managers must handle indoor air quality (IAQ) problems to protect the health and well-being of inhabitants. Poor IAQ can come from several issues, such as poor ventilation, moisture penetration, mold development, or the presence of volatile organic compounds (VOCs).

Property managers must adopt steps to improve IAQ, such as adequate ventilation systems, moisture management, frequent inspections, and rapid removal of mold or other indoor pollutants. Additionally, environmental rules may force property managers to address outside environmental problems such as stormwater management, erosion prevention, and conservation of natural ecosystems. Compliance with these requirements may entail implementing best management practices (BMPs), such as constructing stormwater management systems, erosion control measures, and protecting natural vegetation.

Moreover, property management organizations must comply with legislation pertaining to waste management and recycling. This may include disposing of hazardous waste, recycling items such as paper, plastic, glass, and metal, and complying with municipal recycling rules and programs.

In short, environmental regulations comprise a wide range of rules and regulations that property management organizations must comply with in their day-to-day operations. Knowing and complying with these requirements may help property managers eliminate risks, ensure regulatory compliance, and improve the health and well-being of tenants, property owners, and neighboring communities. Compliance with environmental rules is crucial for property management organizations to sustain ethical standards, retain confidence with stakeholders, and achieve long-term success in the real estate market.

Data Security and Privacy

Property management organizations must consider data security and privacy as they manage sensitive information related to renters, property owners, financial transactions, and property assets. In today's digital era, when data breaches and cyber threats are common, property managers must prioritize the preservation of personal information to defend the privacy and security of their stakeholders.

Property management organizations acquire and keep a significant quantity of personal and financial data from renters, including contact information, rental history, credit reports, and payment details. They also keep sensitive information about property owners, such as property addresses, financial data, and communication logs. Protecting sensitive data against illegal access, abuse, or theft is crucial to preserving confidence and integrity inside the firm.

To maintain data security and privacy, property management organizations must establish comprehensive security measures and adhere to industry best practices. This includes:

1. **Secure Data Storage and Management:**
   Property managers should implement secure databases and cloud storage systems with encryption and access restrictions. Develop data retention rules that specify the duration for which data should be held and the appropriate time for its safe removal.

2. **Access Control and Authentication:**
   Implementing stringent access controls and authentication procedures guarantees that only authorized workers have access to sensitive data. This involves utilizing strong passwords, multi-factor authentication, and role-based access restrictions to limit access to specific personnel depending on their job duties.

3. **Regular Security Audits and Assessments:**
   Property management organizations should undertake regular security audits and assessments to discover weaknesses in their systems and procedures. This may comprise penetration testing, vulnerability scanning, and security risk

assessments to proactively detect and resolve possible security risks.

4. **Employee Training and Awareness:**

    Training staff on data security best practices and raising awareness about the importance of data privacy may help reduce human errors and security breaches. Employees should be taught how to manage sensitive information, spot phishing efforts, and report security breaches quickly.

5. **Compliance with Data Protection Requirements:**
    Property management organizations must comply with appropriate data protection requirements, such as the General Data Protection Regulation (GDPR) in the European Union or the California Consumer Privacy Act (CCPA) in California. Compliance with these requirements entails gaining consent for data collection, issuing visible privacy notifications, and adopting steps to secure personal data.

6. **Secure Communication Channels:**
    Property managers should utilize secure communication channels, such as encrypted email and messaging platforms, when communicating

sensitive information with renters, property owners, and third-party suppliers. This helps prevent the unauthorized interception of private data during transmission.

7. **Incident Response and Data Breach Management:**

    Property management organizations should have a written incident response strategy in place to handle data breaches and security issues efficiently. This includes protocols for alerting impacted persons, regulatory bodies, and law enforcement, as well as efforts to reduce the effect of the breach and avoid future breaches.

Strategies for Risk Mitigation

Risk mitigation methods are crucial for property management organizations to identify, analyze, and handle any hazards that might damage their operations, financial stability, reputation, and stakeholders. By employing effective risk mitigation measures, property management organizations can proactively manage risks and limit their impact on the business.

Comprehensive tenant screening and selection is an important risk reduction method for property management organizations. By completing complete background checks, confirming income and employment, and examining rental history, property managers may limit the risk of leasing to tenants who may default on rent payments, cause property damage, or participate in disruptive behavior. Additionally, having precise lease agreements with defined terms and conditions helps safeguard the rights of both renters and property owners and decreases the probability of conflicts.

Another key risk reduction method is frequent property maintenance and inspection. Property managers should set routine maintenance schedules, conduct frequent inspections, and swiftly handle any maintenance concerns to avoid property damage, ensure tenant safety, and maintain the property's value.

By proactively addressing maintenance concerns, property managers may decrease the likelihood of costly repairs, tenant discontent, and legal penalties.

Risk mitigation also involves financial planning and budgeting. Property management organizations should produce precise financial predictions, set contingency funds for unanticipated needs, and maintain accurate accounting records to track income and spending. By properly managing funds and sticking to budgetary limitations, property managers can reduce the risk of financial instability and maintain the firm's long-term financial health by properly managing funds and adhering to budgetary limitations.

Additionally, property management organizations should incorporate insurance coverage to defend against any risks and liabilities. This may include general liability insurance, property insurance, professional liability insurance (for errors and omissions), and workers' compensation insurance. By having sufficient insurance coverage in place, property managers may limit the financial effects of accidents, property damage, litigation, and other unanticipated events.

Legal compliance is another key part of risk minimization for property management organizations. Property managers must be knowledgeable about applicable federal, state, and local rules and regulations affecting property management activities, including fair housing laws, landlord-tenant laws, environmental regulations, and data privacy laws. By maintaining compliance with applicable rules and regulations, property managers may limit the risk of legal challenges, fines, and penalties.

Effective communication and dispute resolution are also crucial risk reduction methods for property management organizations. Property managers should maintain open and transparent communication with renters, property owners, vendors, and other stakeholders to handle issues, settle conflicts, and prevent misunderstandings. By building strong connections and handling concerns swiftly and effectively, property managers may decrease the risk of tenant discontent, poor reviews, and reputational harm.

Property management organizations should build emergency preparation strategies to limit the risk of catastrophes and natural disasters. This involves designing evacuation strategies, preserving emergency contact information, and adopting steps to safeguard property and assure tenant safety during crises such as fires, floods, or severe weather occurrences.

Effective risk mitigation measures are critical for property management organizations to detect, analyze, and handle possible hazards proactively. By implementing thorough tenant screening, conducting regular property maintenance, managing finances effectively, obtaining appropriate insurance coverage, ensuring legal compliance, fostering communication, and preparing for emergencies, property management businesses can mitigate risks and safeguard the interests of their stakeholders.

Chapter 10.

Building Client Relationships

Developing good customer connections is critical to the success of any property management firm. Cultivating trust, understanding customer needs, offering outstanding service, and maintaining open communication are all essential components of effective client relationship management. Prioritizing client connections may help property management companies increase customer satisfaction, retain clients, create recommendations, and repeat business.

Establishing trust and credibility is an important step in developing client relationships. Property managers must be professional, honest, and dependable in their relationships with clients. This includes keeping promises, delivering on commitments, and being open and honest in all conversations. By continually displaying integrity, property managers may gain their clients' trust and develop long-term partnerships built on mutual respect and trust.

Understanding clients' requirements and preferences is another critical component of good client relationship management. Property managers should listen to their clients, grasp their objectives and priorities, and personalize their services to their individual requirements.

This may include completing detailed property appraisals, discussing client objectives, and tailoring management strategies to meet client expectations. Property managers may reinforce and surpass their clients' expectations by displaying a thorough awareness of their needs and providing unique solutions.

Providing outstanding service is essential for developing and sustaining good client connections. Property managers should endeavor to provide excellent service at all stages, from initial inquiries to ongoing property management services. This includes responding to client queries and requests, resolving issues quickly and effectively, and going above and beyond to provide outstanding value. Property managers may separate themselves from competition by constantly offering exceptional service, earning their clients' loyalty and happiness.

Open and transparent communication is also required to establish effective client relationships. Property managers should communicate with their customers on a frequent basis, updating them on property performance, financial statements, and any difficulties or concerns that may arise. This might include frequent meetings, phone calls, emails, or other kinds of contact, depending on the client's preferences. By keeping customers informed and active in the management process, property managers may build confidence and collaboration while also ensuring alignment with client goals and expectations.

Regularly soliciting input from clients is critical for developing strong connections and always improving service delivery. Property managers should routinely request customer input on their experiences, preferences, and areas for improvement. This might include completing customer satisfaction surveys, scheduling feedback meetings, or just soliciting comments during routine contacts. Constantly listening to and incorporating customer input into their operations, property managers can demonstrate their dedication to client happiness and consistently improve their services.

Developing customer connections entails maintaining continual contact and participation after the original transaction. Property managers should aim to build long-term relationships with their customers by staying in touch, sharing useful insights and resources, and providing support and assistance as needed. This might include sending out frequent newsletters or updates, organizing client gratitude events, or giving instructional resources on property management themes. Property managers may create loyalty and strengthen relationships with customers over time by being involved and exhibiting a genuine interest in their success.

Effective communication.

Effective communication is critical to any property management company's success. It includes not just the exchange of information but also the capacity to communicate clearly, actively listen, and develop strong relationships with clients, renters, vendors, and other stakeholders.

Mastering this talent is critical in the property management profession, where efficient communication may mean the difference between a smooth-running property and one plagued by problems.

First and foremost, successful communication requires clear and precise messaging. Property managers must be able to communicate their ideas, instructions, and expectations in an understandable manner to others. This involves using straightforward language, eliminating jargon or technical phrases where unnecessary, and offering context or clarification when needed. By improving communication clarity, property managers may reduce the likelihood of misunderstandings, mistakes, and confrontations.

Active listening is another important component of good communication. Property managers must pay close attention to the wants, concerns, and input of their clients, renters, and other stakeholders. This includes paying full attention to the speaker, asking clarifying questions, and empathizing with their point of view. Active listening allows property managers to gather useful insights, establish relationships with stakeholders, and demonstrate their dedication to understanding and meeting their requirements.

In addition to verbal communication, nonverbal communication is important for effectively delivering messages. Property managers must be aware of their body language, facial emotions, and gestures while engaging with people.

Positive body language, such as keeping eye contact, nodding in agreement, and exuding a friendly manner, may help express warmth, transparency, and professionalism. Negative body language, such as crossed arms or a scowl, can impede efficient communication and weaken relationships with stakeholders.

Successful communication in property management goes beyond person-to-person contacts and includes textual communication as well. Property managers must be skilled in writing communication, including emails, memoranda, reports, and other written materials. This requires utilizing appropriate syntax, punctuation, and spelling, as well as structuring information in a clear and cohesive manner. Whether creating lease agreements, responding to maintenance requests, or delivering updates to customers, property managers must ensure their written communication is professional, accurate, and easily comprehensible.

Top notch property management communication also entails timely and proactive communication. Property managers must be attentive to queries, requests, and difficulties from customers, renters, and suppliers. This includes swiftly responding to phone calls and emails, addressing maintenance problems in a timely manner, and keeping stakeholders informed of any important updates or developments. By being proactive and responsive in communication, property managers may create trust in their stakeholders and demonstrate their dedication to providing good service.

Additionally, successful communication also requires customizing communication style and strategy for diverse stakeholders. Property managers must be adaptive in their communication approach, taking into account the preferences, personalities, and cultural backgrounds of their audience. This may entail modifying the tone, phrasing, and level of formality to better meet the requirements and preferences of each individual or group. By adapting communication to the individual needs of stakeholders, property managers may develop deeper connections and ensure successful cooperation.

Excellent communication is vital for the success of property management firms. By mastering clear and concise messaging, active listening, positive non-verbal communication, proficient written communication, timely and proactive communication, and an adaptive communication style, property managers can build strong relationships, minimize misunderstandings, and deliver exceptional service to their clients, tenants, and other stakeholders.

Client Retention Strategies

Client retention is essential for any property management firm's long-term success. By employing efficient client retention tactics, property management businesses may develop loyalty, improve connections, and optimize their clients' lifetime value.

These tactics incorporate proactive communication, individualized service, proactive problem-solving, and continual value delivery.

One major method for client retention is maintaining constant communication with clients. Property managers should remain in touch with clients through multiple channels, including phone calls, emails, newsletters, and in-person meetings. Regular communication helps property managers keep customers updated about property updates, market trends, and other pertinent industry news. By continuously being involved with customers, property managers may demonstrate their dedication to their success and develop the connection over time.

Personalized service is another key part of client retention. Property managers should take the time to learn each client's individual needs, preferences, and goals. By adapting their services to match the individual objectives of each customer, property managers may provide a more customized and valued experience. This may entail tailoring management strategies, providing additional services based on customer needs, or providing specific accommodations as necessary. By delivering individualized service, property managers may separate themselves from competitors and boost customer satisfaction and loyalty.

Proactive problem-solving is vital for maintaining clients in the property management profession.

Property managers should anticipate any difficulties or obstacles that may arise and take proactive action to address them before they become major concerns. This may entail doing frequent property inspections, addressing maintenance concerns immediately, and implementing preventative maintenance methods to reduce future problems. By being proactive in problem-solving, property managers may demonstrate their attention to customer pleasure and minimize interruptions to the client's property investment.

Continuous value delivery is also critical for retaining customers. Property managers should always explore opportunities to add value to their services and surpass customer expectations. This may entail supplying extra services, such as landscaping or remodeling services, negotiating competitive vendor contracts to decrease expenditures, or providing educational tools to assist customers in making educated decisions about their properties. Property managers may reinforce the client's opinion of their business's worth and improve the client's loyalty over time by continually providing value.

Building strong relationships with clients is essential for client retention. Property managers should devote time and effort to developing genuine relationships with their clients, founded on trust, transparency, and mutual respect. This requires having a proactive interest in the client's success, actively listening to their issues, and giving compassionate assistance when required. By creating good connections, property managers may generate a sense of loyalty and trust that makes it more probable for customers to continue working with them in the long run.

Asking for input from clients is vital for client retention. Property managers should routinely solicit input from their clients regarding their experiences, preferences, and areas for improvement. This may entail performing client satisfaction surveys, scheduling feedback meetings, or just asking for comments during frequent contacts. By actively listening to customer input and taking action to resolve their problems, property managers may demonstrate their dedication to client happiness and improve the client's loyalty to their firm.

Customer retention is critical to the success of property management organizations. By implementing effective client retention strategies such as regular communication, personalized service, proactive problem-solving, continuous value delivery, building strong relationships, and soliciting feedback, property managers can foster loyalty, strengthen relationships, and maximize their clients' lifetime value.

Managing Complaints and Issues

Handling complaints and concerns properly is vital for preserving great relationships with clients, renters, and other stakeholders in the property management industry. Property managers must tackle complaints and difficulties with sensitivity, professionalism, and a dedication to finding mutually beneficial solutions. By employing efficient tactics for resolving complaints and difficulties, property management organizations may settle disagreements, minimize possible hazards, and boost overall client satisfaction.

Property managers should create clear channels of communication for receiving and addressing complaints and difficulties. This may involve putting up separate phone lines, email addresses, or internet portals where clients and renters may report their problems. By providing easily accessible channels for communication, property managers may encourage stakeholders to raise their concerns quickly, allowing for rapid resolution of issues.

The Property managers should respond swiftly and address the concern presented when a complaint or issue develops. A prompt answer displays attentiveness and a commitment to solve the issue in a timely way. Acknowledging the worry displays empathy and affirms the stakeholder's perspective, which may help reduce tensions and establish rapport.

After acknowledging a complaint or concern, property managers should thoroughly examine the situation to determine the root cause and collect pertinent evidence. This may require interviewing concerned individuals, analyzing paperwork, or doing site inspections, depending on the severity of the issue. By performing a comprehensive investigation, property managers can acquire sufficient information to design a successful resolution approach.

During evaluation of the complaint or issue, property managers should communicate their findings and possible remedies to the relevant stakeholders. Clear and honest communication is crucial at this stage to ensure that all parties understand the proposed resolution and agree on the following steps. Property managers should also set realistic timetables for fixing the issue and keep stakeholders informed of any progress or delays.

When suggesting solutions to complaints or challenges, property managers should prioritize creating mutually beneficial results that meet the concerns presented while aligning with the interests of all parties involved. This may entail negotiating concessions, giving alternative options, or paying compensation when appropriate. By exploring win-win solutions, property managers may promote goodwill and preserve strong relationships with stakeholders.

Throughout the resolution process, property managers should show professionalism and stay calm, especially in stressful situations. It is crucial to handle complaints and difficulties with empathy and respect, regardless of the circumstances. By exhibiting professionalism and empathy, property managers may help de-escalate situations and develop trust with stakeholders.

Property managers should follow up with stakeholders after addressing a complaint or issue to confirm that the resolution was satisfactory and that any necessary follow-up measures have been completed. Following up indicates a commitment to client satisfaction and gives a chance to resolve any remaining issues or queries.

Finally, property managers should document any complaints and difficulties, including the methods taken to address them and the outcomes reached. Keeping accurate records of complaints and issue resolution helps property managers evaluate trends, identify reoccurring concerns, and adopt preventative actions to reduce future problems.

Chapter 11

Scaling Your Property Management Business

Scaling a property management firm entails expanding operations, boosting efficiency, and raising income while maintaining high-quality service and customer satisfaction. As property management firms develop, they confront new issues and opportunities that demand strategic planning, inventive solutions, and successful execution. Here's a full analysis of essential issues for expanding a property management business:

Expanding service offerings:
One technique for expanding a property management firm is to extend service offerings to attract more clients and enhance income sources. This may entail providing additional property management services, such as gardening, renovation management, or real estate investment advice. By broadening their service offerings, property management organizations may appeal to a larger customer base and win greater market share.

Implementing technological solutions:
Technology plays a significant role in expanding a property management firm by simplifying processes, boosting productivity, and improving the customer experience. Property management software, for example, may automate regular duties such as rent collection, maintenance requests, and tenant contacts, allowing property managers to handle

larger portfolios with less staff. Additionally, employing data analytics solutions may give important insights into market trends, tenant preferences, and property performance, enabling informed decision-making and strategic planning.

Optimizing processes and workflows:
Efficient procedures and workflows are vital for expanding a property management organization. Streamlining administrative duties, standardizing procedures, and applying best practices may enhance productivity and minimize operating expenses. Property managers should routinely analyze and optimize their procedures to discover opportunities for improvement and eliminate bottlenecks that may hamper scalability.

Building a Reliable Team:
As a property management firm expands, it's vital to create a solid team of qualified experts that can efficiently handle the rising workload and customer needs. Hiring competent people, offering continuing training and professional development opportunities, and maintaining a pleasant work culture are vital for recruiting and retaining top talent. A well-trained and motivated workforce is crucial to delivering high-quality service and retaining customer satisfaction as the firm expands.

Developing Strategic Partnerships:
Strategic connections with real estate agents, contractors, vendors, and other industry specialists may help property management organizations expand more successfully. Collaborating with trustworthy partners may give access to extra resources, experience, and networking opportunities,

helping the organization grow its reach and capabilities. By forming mutually beneficial collaborations, property management organizations can leverage synergies and generate value for their clients and stakeholders.

Implementing growth strategies:
To scale successfully, property management organizations must establish and implement growth plans that correspond with their long-term objectives. This may entail targeting certain market categories, expanding into new geographic locations, or purchasing rivals to boost market share. Strategic planning, market research, and financial analysis are critical for identifying development possibilities and executing effective expansion initiatives.

Maintaining client relationships:
While concentrating on development and expansion, it's vital for property management organizations to emphasize maintaining great client connections and offering outstanding service. Client satisfaction is crucial for maintaining existing clients and acquiring new ones through recommendations and positive word-of-mouth. Property managers should continue to contact customers regularly, answer their wants and complaints immediately, and seek to exceed their expectations at every opportunity.

Monitoring Performance and Metrics:
Effective scaling needs continual monitoring of key performance metrics and business indicators to measure progress, identify areas for improvement, and make data-driven choices. Property managers should frequently monitor financial performance, customer satisfaction ratings, occupancy rates, and other pertinent data to

determine the health and growth trajectory of the firm. This data-driven strategy enables property management organizations to course-correct as needed and improve their strategies for continuous scalability and profitability.

In short, expanding a property management firm takes careful planning, intelligent decision-making, and a dedication to delivering high-quality service. By expanding service offerings, leveraging technology, optimizing processes, building a reliable team, developing strategic partnerships, implementing growth strategies, maintaining client relationships, and monitoring performance metrics, property management businesses can effectively scale their operations while maintaining client satisfaction and achieving long-term success.

Expansion Strategies

Expanding a property management firm involves a well-thought-out plan that examines numerous elements such as market dynamics, client demands, competition, and available resources. Successful expansion strategies require finding development possibilities, creating clear targets, and implementing plans successfully. Here's a full analysis of expansion methods for property management businesses:

1. **Market Analysis**:
Before growing, it's vital to undertake a full market study to discover development prospects and examine the competitive environment. Analyze demographic trends,

rental market dynamics, economic data, and local legislation to establish the possibility of growth in new geographic regions. Evaluate the demand for property management services and the presence of competitors to identify untapped areas or specialized sectors with growth potential.

2. Geographic Expansion:

One strategy for property management organizations is geographic expansion, which entails entering new markets or expanding operations into surrounding areas. Consider aspects such as population growth, rental demand, job possibilities, and real estate market trends when selecting target sites for expansion. Establishing a physical presence in new areas may necessitate creating branch offices or collaborating with local real estate specialists to simplify market entry and develop a reputation.

3. Portfolio Diversification:

Diversifying the property management portfolio by offering more services or managing different types of properties helps accelerate corporate development. Consider expanding into additional property categories such as commercial real estate, holiday rentals, or affordable housing to widen the customer base and grasp market possibilities. Offering value-added services such as property maintenance, renovation management, or real estate investment advice may help boost income streams and differentiate the firm from competition.

4. Strategic Partnerships:

Collaborating with strategic partners helps speed expansion by using existing networks, resources, and skills. Establish alliances with real estate brokers, property developers, investors, and industry groups to obtain access to new clients, assets, and market information. Joint ventures, referral agreements, and co-marketing campaigns can help property management organizations expand their reach and penetrate new market segments more efficiently.

5. Acquisitions and mergers:
Acquiring or merging with existing property management firms can be a strategic growth strategy for increasing market presence and consolidating market dominance. Identify possible acquisition targets or merger prospects that match the existing company model and fit with expansion plans. Acquiring established enterprises with a loyal client base, experienced staff, and significant assets can give a shortcut to growth and boost the business's competitive position in the market.

6. Online Presence and Digital Marketing:
Investing in digital marketing tactics and building a strong online presence is vital for growing the reach and visibility of a property management firm. Develop a professional website, develop compelling content, and harness social media channels to attract new clients and display the company's services and skills. Implement search engine optimization (SEO) tactics to boost your online presence and generate leads from prospective property owners and investors.

7. Brand Building and Reputation Management:
Building a strong brand identity and reputation is vital for acquiring clients and differentiating the firm in a competitive market. Invest in branding initiatives to express

the company's principles, strengths, and unique selling propositions effectively. Deliver great service, emphasize customer happiness, and aggressively request client feedback to maintain a favorable reputation and establish trust with clients, renters, and industry stakeholders.

8. Scalable Infrastructure and Systems:
To enable expansion, invest in scalable infrastructure and systems that can manage the growing workload and client base effectively. Implement property management software, customer relationship management (CRM) systems, and automated workflows to simplify operations, boost efficiency, and enhance service delivery. Scalable infrastructure guarantees that the firm can withstand expansion without compromising quality or performance.

Expansion plans for property management organizations comprise a combination of market study, regional expansion, portfolio diversification, strategic alliances, acquisitions, digital marketing, brand promotion, and scalable infrastructure. By recognizing growth possibilities, defining clear targets, and implementing expansion plans intelligently, property management organizations may achieve sustainable growth and long-term success in the competitive real estate market.

Diversification of Services

Diversification of services is a strategic method that property management organizations can pursue to increase their capabilities beyond typical property management tasks. By expanding their services, these organizations can meet the changing demands of clients, differentiate themselves in a competitive market, and develop alternative income sources. Here's a full discussion of how property management organizations might diversify their services:

1. Additional Property Management Services:
Property management organizations might start by offering other services that complement their main property management activities. These services may include property upkeep, gardening, cleaning, and repair services. By providing complete property care solutions, businesses may boost the value proposition for customers and attract property owners searching for one-stop-shop solutions for their real estate assets.

2. Real Estate Investment Consulting:
Offering real estate investment advisory services may be an efficient way for property management organizations to expand their offerings. This comprises providing customers with expert advice on property investment strategies, market trends, property valuation, and portfolio management. By using their expertise of the local real estate market and investing concepts, property management businesses may assist clients in making educated investment decisions and maximizing their real estate portfolios.

3. Vacation Rental Management:
Diversifying into vacation rental management helps property management organizations tap into the rising market for short-term rentals and vacation properties. This service entails managing vacation rental homes on behalf of

owners, processing guest bookings, managing reservations, organizing cleaning and maintenance, and ensuring regulatory compliance. By catering to the demands of vacation home owners, businesses may extend their customer base and income potential.

4. **Commercial Property Management:**
Expanding into commercial property management gives property management organizations the ability to manage a varied range of assets, including office buildings, retail centers, and industrial complexes. Commercial property management services may encompass lease negotiations, tenant interactions, facility management, and financial reporting. By branching into commercial property management, firms may reach a new section of the real estate market and profit from the need for professional management services.

5. **Community Association Management:**
Community association management comprises managing homeowner associations (HOAs), condominium associations, and cooperative housing complexes. This service comprises administrative chores, financial management, property upkeep, compliance with governing documents, and community participation. By offering community association management services, property management organizations may cater to the demands of residential communities and create long-term partnerships with homeowner associations.

6. **Real Estate Brokerage Services:**
Diversifying into real estate brokerage services helps property management organizations ease property

transactions and purchases for customers. This comprises representing buyers and sellers in real estate transactions, performing market research, promoting properties, negotiating deals, and assisting in the closing process. By adding brokerage services to their portfolio, property management organizations may offer full real estate solutions and make additional money through commissions.

7. **Legal and Compliance Services:**
Providing legal and regulatory services relating to property management might be another opportunity for diversification. This may involve lease preparation and review, eviction processes, regulatory compliance, and dispute resolution services. By delivering legal advice and maintaining compliance with local legislation, property management services may decrease risks for property owners and boost their value proposition.

Diversifying services helps property management organizations increase their products, serve a greater range of clients, and establish new revenue sources. By discovering additional services, using their knowledge, and reacting to market demands, property management businesses can increase their competitive position and achieve sustainable development in the real estate industry.

Franchising Opportunities

Franchising provides an attractive alternative for businesses wishing to enter the property management sector or grow an existing firm. It gives a unique chance to harness an existing brand, proven business strategy, and continuous support system while maintaining a degree of autonomy and freedom.

Let's go into a comprehensive analysis of franchising potential in the property management sector:

Benefits of Franchising:

Franchising offers numerous appealing benefits for anyone seeking to establish a property management business, including:

1. **Established Brand Awareness:** Franchising allows entrepreneurs to benefit from the established brand awareness of the franchisor. This may drastically minimize the time and resources necessary to create brand awareness and reputation in the competitive property management industry.

2. **Proven Business Plan:** Franchisors often supply franchisees with a proven business plan that has been tested and modified over time. This comprises established operating processes, marketing tactics, and technological systems meant to improve corporate performance and profitability.

3. **Training and assistance:** Franchisees receive thorough training and continuous assistance from the franchisor. This comprises initial training programs covering all elements of property management operations, as well as continual assistance, mentorship, and access to resources to help navigate hurdles and achieve success.

4. **Access to Technology and Tools:** Franchisees have access to proprietary technology platforms, software systems, and tools developed by the franchisor. These solutions expedite property management operations, promote efficiency, and improve customer satisfaction.

5. **Economies of Scale:** Franchising allows entrepreneurs to profit from economies of scale in purchasing, marketing, and administrative operations. By combining resources with other franchisees within the network, franchisees may receive cheaper pricing on supplies, services, and advertising, thereby enhancing profitability.

6. **Network and Collaboration:** Joining a franchise network gives access to a community of like-minded experts within the property management business. This network fosters cooperation, information exchange, and peer support, enabling franchisees to benefit from one another's experiences and best practices.

Considerations for franchisees

While franchising offers enticing advantages, potential franchisees should carefully assess many criteria before committing to a franchise opportunity:

1. **Franchise Fees and Royalties:** Franchisees are often expected to pay an initial franchise fee and periodic royalties to the franchisor. It's critical to understand the price structure, including any additional expenditures such as marketing or technology fees, and analyze the financial consequences for the organization.

2. **Territorial Rights:** Franchise agreements frequently include territorial rights that specify the geographic region in which the franchisee can operate. It's vital to establish the exclusivity of the territory and any constraints on expansion inside or beyond the territory.

3. **Franchise Agreement Terms:** Franchisees must carefully evaluate the terms and conditions of the franchise agreement, including the duration of the agreement, renewal possibilities, termination provisions, and duties relating to branding, marketing, and operations.

4. **Support and Training:** Assess the degree of support and training given by the franchisor, including the availability of field support representatives, continuing training programs, and access to operational resources. Ensure that the franchisor is committed to aiding franchisees in attaining their business goals.

5. **Brand Reputation and Compliance:** Research the reputation of the franchisor within the property management sector and check its compliance with relevant laws, regulations, and industry standards. A solid brand reputation and dedication to ethical business practices are vital for long-term success.

Franchising is a great option for entrepreneurs interested in entering the property management industry or growing their existing firm. People who work with a respected franchisor may benefit from brand awareness, established business models, thorough training and support, and access to technology and resources. However, it's crucial for potential franchisees to undertake full due diligence, examine the conditions of the franchise agreement, and establish compatibility with their business goals and values before making a commitment. With careful analysis and strategic preparation, franchising may be a feasible road to success in the dynamic and competitive property management business.

Chapter 12

Staying informed and adapting to changes

Staying knowledgeable and adaptive are vital attributes for success in any business, especially in the ever-evolving world of property management. Let's discuss how remaining informed and adjusting to changes might assist your property management business:

Continuous learning and education:

Staying informed begins with a dedication to constant learning and education. This requires staying aware of industry trends, best practices, and regulatory developments that affect the property management business. By attending conferences, workshops, and seminars and participating in industry groups and networking events, property managers may learn useful insights, extend their knowledge base, and stay ahead of the curve.

Monitoring Market Trends:

In the dynamic property management sector, market trends can move swiftly owing to variables such as demographic shifts, economic situations, and technological improvements. Property managers must proactively analyze market trends, including rental prices, occupancy rates, and tenant preferences, to make educated decisions regarding property purchases, pricing tactics, and service offers.

Adopting Technology Solutions:

Technology plays a vital role in contemporary property management, delivering new solutions to simplify operations, enhance tenant experiences, and improve efficiency. Property managers should embrace digital solutions such as property management software, online payment systems, and smart building technologies to improve workflows, automate regular operations, and give greater services to customers and renters.

Embracing Sustainability Practices:

With rising awareness of environmental concerns, sustainability has become an important element in property management. Property managers should be knowledgeable about sustainable practices and green building projects that may decrease operational costs, boost property value, and attract environmentally conscious renters. Adopting energy-efficient equipment, introducing recycling programs, and encouraging sustainable living habits may differentiate your property management firm and correspond with shifting consumer demands.

Navigating Regulatory Changes:

The property management landscape is subject to different rules and legislation that can affect operations and compliance obligations. Property managers must stay informed about changes in landlord-tenant legislation, fair housing standards, and property maintenance requirements to ensure legal compliance and minimize potential hazards. Regularly evaluating and amending lease agreements, property regulations, and maintenance protocols is vital to respond to legislative changes and safeguard the interests of property owners and renters.

Flexibility and adaptability:

In a dynamic and competitive sector like property management, flexibility and adaptation are crucial. Property managers must be prepared to pivot and adapt their tactics in response to changing market conditions, developing technology, and growing client demands. By embracing a philosophy of constant improvement and adaptability, property managers may position themselves for long-term success and stay resilient in the face of unpredictability.

Staying educated and adaptive is key to success in the property management sector. By committing to continuous learning, tracking market trends, embracing technology, implementing sustainable practices, managing regulatory changes, and displaying flexibility, property managers may remain ahead of the curve and prosper in a continually developing industrial landscape. Property managers who are educated and adaptive may increase operational efficiency, provide excellent services, and achieve sustainable development for their property management firm.

Industry Updates and Trends

Keeping up with industry developments and trends is vital for being competitive and educated in the property management industry. Let's look into the relevance of industry updates and trends:

Market Insights:

Industry updates give useful insights into market dynamics, including variations in property valuations, rental rates, and occupancy patterns. By remaining current on market changes, property managers may make educated judgments about property acquisitions, pricing tactics, and investment possibilities.

Technology Integration:

The property management sector is constantly expanding with technological advancements. Industry updates emphasize new software platforms, smart building technology, and digital marketing trends that may boost operational efficiency and tenant experiences. Property managers may harness these technologies to streamline operations, increase communication, and distinguish their services in the marketplace.

Regulatory Changes:

Property management is subject to different rules and legislation that might affect operations and compliance needs. Industry updates keep property managers informed about changes in landlord-tenant legislation, fair housing standards, and property maintenance guidelines. Staying current on regulatory changes assures legal compliance and mitigates possible hazards for property owners and tenants.

Tenant Preferences:

Industry updates give insight on shifting tenant preferences and lifestyle trends that impact property management techniques. From facilities like fitness centers and pet-friendly rules to sustainability efforts and community participation programs, researching tenant preferences helps property managers adjust their services to meet the requirements and expectations of modern tenants.

Competitive Landscape:

Monitoring industry updates helps property managers stay updated about rivals' tactics, market positioning, and service offers. By examining rivals' strengths and shortcomings, property managers may uncover possibilities for differentiation and establish distinct value propositions that appeal to property owners and renters.

Emerging Markets and Opportunities:

Industry updates emphasize expanding markets, investment possibilities, and developing trends that property managers may profit from. Property managers uncover new revenue sources and strategically expand their portfolio by staying updated on industry trends, including the emergence of co-living spaces, short-term rental markets, and specialty property sectors like elder housing or student accommodations.

Networking and Collaboration:

Attending industry events, conferences, and networking opportunities offered by industry updates enables property managers to meet with peers, industry experts, and possible partners. These networking events stimulate cooperation, information exchange, and professional growth, eventually boosting the property management community and fostering innovation within the sector.

Professional Development

Professional development is a critical part of success in the property management sector. Let's talk about why it's important and how property managers can benefit from constant learning and growth:

Continuous Learning:

Property management is a comprehensive job that demands a wide skill set spanning topics such as leasing, maintenance, financial administration, and customer service. Professional development programs, such as workshops, seminars, and online courses, enable property managers to expand their knowledge and abilities in these areas. Property remaining current on industry best practices, legislation, and emerging trends, property managers can offer high-quality services and respond to growing market needs efficiently.

Career Advancement:

Engaging in professional development can create opportunities for career advancement in the property management industry. Property managers that actively pursue additional credentials, such as the Certified Property Manager (CPM) designation or the National Apartment Leasing Professional (NALP) accreditation, exhibit a dedication to quality and continual development. These certifications may strengthen their credibility, raise their marketability, and open the road for career growth into leadership roles or higher-level positions within property management organizations.

Enhanced Client Relationships:

Professional development not only helps property managers but also promotes client relationships. Clients, whether property owners or renters, want property managers to be educated, professional, and dependable in managing their assets. By investing in continual training and development, property managers may create trust with their customers, demonstrate their knowledge, and deliver excellent service that surpasses expectations. Strong client connections are vital for customer retention, referrals, and long-term company success in the competitive property management sector.

Adaptability and Innovation:

The property management sector is continually developing, driven by technological breakthroughs, regulatory changes, and altering market trends. Property managers that engage in continual professional development are better positioned to respond to these changes and welcome innovation within their operations. Whether it's adopting new property management software, implementing sustainable practices, or embracing digital marketing methods, professionals who value learning and growth may position themselves as industry leaders and stay ahead of the curve.

Networking and Collaboration:

Professional development initiatives also enable networking and collaboration within the property management sector. Attending professional conferences, workshops, and networking events helps property managers engage with peers, industry experts, and new business partners. These relationships give significant insights, assistance, and chances for collaboration, such as sharing best practices, trading recommendations, and exploring collaborative ventures. Networking boosts professional progress and develops a sense of community within the property management sector.

Adapting to Market Changes

Adapting to market changes is a vital component of running a successful property management firm. Here's a full explanation of why adaptability is necessary and how property managers may effectively handle evolving market dynamics:

Market Dynamics:

The property management sector operates within a dynamic market driven by several elements, such as economic conditions, demographic trends, technology improvements, regulatory changes, and adjustments in customer preferences. These trends can affect demand for rental homes, property valuations, rental rates, and the overall competitiveness of the market. Property managers must be aware of these developments in order to make informed decisions and adjust their strategies accordingly.

Customer Needs and Preferences:

Tenant tastes and expectations evolve over time, influenced by lifestyle, demography, and technology. To attract and retain renters, property managers must recognize and respond to these evolving tastes. For example, younger generations may emphasize amenities like smart home technology and sustainability elements, while others may favor convenience and community facilities.

Property managers that proactively recognize and respond to these developing demands may sustain high occupancy rates and tenant satisfaction.

Technological Advancements:

Advancements in technology have altered the property management sector, enabling novel solutions for communication, marketing, property upkeep, and tenant management. Property managers must embrace this technology to streamline operations, boost efficiency, and enhance the tenant experience. This may involve adopting property management software, introducing online rental platforms, leveraging digital marketing methods, and adding smart home gadgets to increase property security and efficiency.

Regulatory Changes:

Property management is subject to different municipal, state, and federal rules that can affect how properties are managed and leased. Changes in legislation, zoning rules, landlord-tenant restrictions, and housing policies can greatly alter property management methods. To managers must keep updated about these regulatory developments and assure compliance to prevent legal complications and financial fines.

Competitive Landscape:

The property management sector is very competitive, with multiple organizations vying for customers and renters. Property managers must regularly examine the competitive landscape, watch rivals' strategies, and seek opportunities for distinction. This may entail introducing innovative services, increasing customer service, expanding property amenities, or modifying pricing tactics to remain competitive in the market.

Flexibility and Agility:

Adapting to market changes needs flexibility and agility in decision-making and operations. Property managers should be proactive in monitoring market changes, finding opportunities, and adapting their business plans accordingly. This may require updating marketing methods, altering lease terms, optimizing rental prices, or investing in property modifications to correspond with market demand.

Made in the USA
Coppell, TX
04 April 2025